BROCCOLI & COMPANY

Over 100 healthy recipes for broccoli,
Brussels sprouts, cabbage, cauliflower,
collards, kale, kohlrabi, mustard greens,
rutabaga, and turnips

by
Audra and Jack Hendrickson

A Garden Way Publishing Book

STOREY

Storey Communications, Inc.
Schoolhouse Road
Pownal, Vermont 05261

*This book is dedicated
to our teachers and mentors,
our colleagues and friends.*

Front cover photograph by Nick Whitman
Text designed and produced by Nancy Lamb
Drawings #3, 4, 5, 6, 7 on pages 123, 124, 125 by Elayne Sears
Drawings #1, 2 on pages 122, 123 and #1, 2, 3, 4 on page 134 by Alison Kolesar
Chapter opening illustrations and remaining illustrations from Food and Drink
    Spot Illustrations *by Susan Gaber, Dover Publications.*
Edited by Constance Oxley
Typesetting by Accura Type & Design

The name Garden Way Publishing is licensed to Storey Communications, Inc., by Garden Way, Inc.

Printed in the United States by Courier
Sixth printing, July 1993

Library of Congress Cataloging-in-Publication Data

Hendrickson, Audra.
   Broccoli & Company : over 100 recipes for broccoli, Brussels sprouts, cabbage, cauliflower, collards, kale, kohlrabi, mustard greens, rutabaga, and turnips / by Audra and Jack Hendrickson.
   "A Garden Way Publishing book."
   Includes index.
   ISBN 0-88266-558-8 : $7.95
   1. Cookery (Broccoli)   2. Cookery (Vegetables)   3. Brassica.
I. Hendrickson, Jack.   II. Title.   III. Title: Broccoli and company.
TX803.B66H46   1989
641.6'535—dc20

0-88266-558-8 (pb)   89-4533
0-88266-559-6 (hc)   CIP

CONTENTS

FROM THE AUTHORS

THE VEGETABLES THAT comprise *BROCCOLI & COMPANY* are said to have divine origins, with Greek myths tracing them to Zeus himself: Laboring to explain two contradictory oracles, the ruler of the gods perspired, and from that divine perspiration sprang the first *colewort*, the ancestor of the cabbage and the other vegetables in the plant family *cruciferae*.

Hearty and healthful, cabbage, broccoli, and their foremost plant world siblings—Brussels sprouts, cauliflower, collards, kale, kohlrabi, mustard greens, rutabaga, and turnip—have been mainstays in the diets of populations around the globe for thousands of years.

These vegetables are low in calories and low in sodium—good news for those millions of Americans who are on low calorie and/or sodium-restricted diets. They are virtually fat-free, with no cholesterol. They contain the bulk and fiber nutrition experts credit with reducing many intestinal disorders.

Small wonder, then, that the vegetables that comprise *BROCCOLI & COMPANY* and are known as *cruciferae*, because of the cross- or cruciform-shaped blossoms they produce, are thought by many to be humanity's foremost friends in the plant world. Few others are as rich in essential vitamins, vital minerals, and food value. Few others are as adaptable to a wide range of seasons, climates, and soils. Few others are as tough, tenacious, and resistant to diseases and pests. They can survive under conditions intolerable to most food plants: One variety of cabbage is so hardy it can withstand temperatures as low as zero degrees Fahrenheit!

It is easy to grow your own Broccoli & Company vegetables, but if you have neither the inclination, the time, nor the space to do so, they are available year-round in supermarkets, they can be stored for weeks in your refrigerator, and they can be frozen, canned, or dried for long-term storage.

The recipes that follow have been compiled, developed, and tested to assist you in making these versatile vegetables a regular part of a healthful daily diet. They include appetizers such as *Quichelettes* and *Brussels Sprouts Veronica*; soups such as *Potage de Navet* and *Danish Dumpling*; salads such as *Company Coleslaw* and *Tossed Beans and Greens*; main dishes such as *Swedish Meatball Cabbage* and *Crash Hash*; side dishes such as *Coliflor Español* and *Punchnep Gold*; luncheon dishes such as *Scramble con Carne* and *Russian Reubens*; and unique desserts such as *Sauerkraut Chocolate Cake* and *Rutabaga Pudding*.

All of them are good. All of them are good for you. All of them are bursting with beta-carotene, vitamin C, minerals, and natural fiber.

God aptit och god hälsa!
Audra and Jack Hendrickson

BROCCOLI & COMPANY:
A Prospectus

Some books are to be tasted,
others to be swallowed,
and some few to be chewed and digested.

—Francis Bacon

They charged them to be careful to treat him well, and to give him such food as was comforting and good for his heart and his brain.

—Cervantes

SCIENTISTS ESTIMATE THAT 35 percent of all cancer deaths may be related to what we eat. In a 1982 report titled "Diet, Nutrition, and Cancer," a blue-ribbon committee assembled by the National Academy of Sciences reported that "consumption of certain vegetables, especially carotene-rich (i.e., dark green and deep yellow) vegetables and cruciferous vegetables (e.g., cabbage, broccoli, cauliflower, and Brussels sprouts) is associated with a reduction in the incidence of cancer at several sites in humans . . . ." Epithelial tissue, where most fatal cancers occur, is particularly affected: the skin and eyes; stomach, intestine, and bladder linings; the inner surface of lungs, bronchial and nasal passages, throat and mouth; and the lining of reproductive organs.

A follow-up was published in 1988—a comprehensive study of the effects of diet on *all* diseases, not just cancer. Broccoli & Company vegetables, because of the variety of their nutritional benefits, were proven as beneficial against diseases in general as they are beneficial against cancer in particular. Such plants are apparently inducers of certain enzymes that detoxify chemicals or inhibit them from becoming carcinogens.

An ongoing study is examining the effects of beta-carotene on lung cancer incidence in particular. Preliminary studies indicate that the effect of beta-carotene will be dramatically positive. One group, whose beta-carotene consumption was above average, had less than half the risk of lung cancer of people in similar circumstances whose consumption of beta-carotene-rich foods was below average.

There is also growing evidence of less risk of most cancers for people who eat foods rich in ascorbic acid (vitamin C), fiber, vitamin E, and selenium.

BETA-CAROTENE (VITAMIN A)

Beta-carotene is a component of dietary vitamin A, one of a family of related chemical substances called "carotenoids" that are important nutritional elements. The carotenes produced by plants are the source of all vitamin A. Carotenes are converted to vitamin A by our bodies when needed, with any excess stored in the liver or fat tissue for later conversion and use, or elimination if the accumulation becomes too great. Adults with diets deficient in beta-carotene (vitamin A) often suffer from night blindness and extreme sensitivity to sunlight. Fingernails split, peel, and become ridged; hair becomes dry, brittle, and dull; and skin dries, wrinkles, and develops blemishes. In children, severe deficiency can result in blindness, increased susceptibility to infection, and retardation of growth, bone, and teeth development.

Broccoli & Company vegetables are rich in beta-carotene though its presence is masked by the chlorophyll that makes these vegetables green. The richness and depth of color in cruciferous vegetables is usually an indication of the amount of beta-carotene they contain. Broccoli, for example, has a lot of beta-carotene, and cauliflower has little. In fact, a single serving of broccoli or one of the greens has enough beta-carotene to provide more than the daily allowance requirement of vitamin A.

In addition to Broccoli & Company vegetables, foods high in beta-carotene include carrots, apricots, yellow peaches, sweet potatoes, winter squash, pumpkin, and other deep yellow vegetables and fruits.

ASCORBIC ACID (VITAMIN C)

Scientific researchers have conducted numerous studies showing that people with diets high in foods containing vitamin C are at lower risk than others for the gastric, esophogeal, and laryngeal cancers that comprise one of twenty new cancer cases, and cause one out of seventeen cancer-related deaths.

Water-soluble vitamin C is found in abundance in Broccoli & Company vegetables and citrus fruits. (See FACTS & FIGURES on page 9, and chart on pages 6-8.) Since it is not stored by the body, adequate amounts of the vitamin must be taken in every day. In addition to its cancer-inhibiting characteristics, ascorbic acid (vitamin C) is essential for skin tone and smoothness; healthy cartilage, bones, and teeth; tissue metabolism; good circulation; prevention of bruising; promotion of healing; and production of the white blood cells that protect against infections and bacterial toxins.

FIBER

Dietary fiber—partially digestible or nondigestible plant cell material—helps move food quickly through the alimentary canal and out of the body, preventing constipation, promoting a healthy digestive tract, and reducing contact time between possible carcinogens in food and the intestines. Some theorize that fiber helps prevent diabetes and gastrointestinal disorders such as diverticular disease, diarrhea, and colon cancer. In countries where high fiber diets are the norm, there are significantly fewer colorectal cancers than in the United States. The American Institute for Cancer Research guidelines call for the consumption of 25-35 grams of fiber a day instead of the 10-20 grams most

Americans now consume. People who eat a wide variety of vegetables, fruits, and whole-grain cereal products likely get enough of the right kinds of fiber. However, those with kidney disease, diabetes, or other serious health problems should consult their physicians before changing their diets. (See chart on pages 6-8 for amounts of fiber contained in Broccoli & Company vegetables.)

VITAMIN E AND SELENIUM

In one international dietary study, mortality rates from colon, rectal, and breast cancers were shown to be lower in countries where foods containing selenium were regularly consumed. In addition, vitamin E and selenium have been found to inhibit skin tumors, and carcinogenesis in a number of tissues. Significant amounts of vitamin E are found in green leafy vegetables such as those which are included in *BROCCOLI & COMPANY*. Scientists speculate that because vitamin E and beta-carotene are fat soluble, while vitamin C is water soluble, such nutrients may complement each other as cancer inhibitors. In fact, some researchers have stated that gastric cancer is a preventable disease whose incidence could perhaps be cut if people daily ate meals including the food elements of vitamins E, beta-carotene, and vitamin C.

CALCIUM, IRON, B-VITAMINS, AND POTASSIUM

Broccoli and other cruciferous vegetables are excellent natural sources of the calcium necessary to maintain healthy bones and prevent osteoporosis. They are good sources of iron, with normal servings providing 10 percent or more of suggested daily requirement amounts. They are also rich in the thiamine and pantothenic acid needed for carbohydrate metabolism and conversion of other foods into energy; the riboflavin and niacin that help regulate metabolism and promote healthy skin; the vitamin B_6, folacin, and B_{12} essential to the formation of red blood cells; and the potassium so important to the maintenance of health.

SODIUM

Broccoli & Company vegetables contain little or no sodium, too much of which may aggravate the high blood pressure afflicting about one in four Americans—some 60 million people. High blood pressure can increase the risk of heart attack, stroke, and kidney disease.

FAT

Dietary fat is thought to increase production in the digestive system of certain bile acids believed to promote colon cancer. Contrarily, bulk produced by dietary fiber is thought to dilute the acids and lower cancer risk. Increasing the amounts of vegetables in our diets lowers the amount of other things we eat, including fat, which also helps in controlling weight. The Food and Drug Administration defines "low fat" as 2 grams of fat or less per serving of any food. (See chart on pages 6-8 for fat content of Broccoli & Company vegetables.)

We advise consulting your physician about a healthful eating plan designed to meet your particular needs. General health and nutrition guidelines include recommendations to:

1. Maintain ideal weight;
2. Exercise regularly;
3. Eat at least three servings daily of vegetables, especially those in the cruciferous family, such as broccoli, Brussels sprouts, and cabbage; and dark green or deep orange vegetables rich in beta-carotene, such as carrots, sweet potatoes, and winter squash;
4. Eat at least three servings daily of fruit, especially citrus fruits and those high in beta-carotene, such as apricots, peaches, and cantaloupe;
5. Eat at least four servings daily of breads, cereals, and starchy foods;
6. Drink at least two cups daily of low-fat milk, or its equivalent;
7. Reduce intake of fat of all kinds—including saturated, polyunsaturated, and monounsaturated —to no more than 30 percent of total daily calories;
8. Use soft margarine made from liquid vegetable oils in place of stick margarines or butter;
9. Avoid foods containing cholesterol;
10. Minimize use of sugar;
11. Minimize use of salt;
12. Minimize consumption of salt-cured, smoked, or salt-pickled foods;
13. Minimize consumption of charcoal-broiled foods;
14. Drink alcohol sparingly or not at all; and
15. Adhere to the recommended daily allowance (RDA) guidelines compiled by the U.S. Food and Drug Administration.

COMPOSITION OF FOODS, 100 GRAMS, EDIBLE PORTION*

[Numbers in parentheses denote values imputed—usually from another form of the food or from a similar food. Zero in parentheses indicates that the amount of a constituent probably is none or is too small to measure. Dashes denote lack of reliable data for a constituent believed to be present in measurable amount. Calculated values as those based on a recipe, are not in parentheses.]

Food and Description	Water	Food energy	Pro-tein	Fat	Carboyhdrate Total	Fiber	Ash	Cal-cium	Phos-phorus	Iron	Sod-ium	Potas-sium	Vitamin A value	Thia-mine	Ribo-flavin	Niacin	Ascor-bic acid
	Percent	Calories	Grams	Grams	Grams	Grams	Grams	Milli-grams	Milli-grams	Milli-grams	Milli-grams	Milli-grams	Inter-national unit	Milli-grams	Milli-grams	Milli-grams	Milli-grams
Broccoli:																	
Raw spears	89.1	32	3.6	.3	5.9	1.5	1.1	103	78	1.1	15	382	2,500	.10	.23	.9	113
Cooked spears, boiled, drained	91.3	26	3.1	.3	4.5	1.5	.8	88	62	.8	10	267	2,500	.09	.20	.8	90
Frozen:																	
Chopped:																	
Not thawed:	90.6	29	3.2	.3	5.2	1.1	.7	58	59	.7	17	241	2,600	.07	.13	.6	70
Cooked, boiled, drained	91.6	26	2.9	.3	4.6	1.1	.6	54	56	.7	15	212	2,600	.06	.12	.5	57
Spears:																	
Not thawed:	90.7	28	3.3	.2	5.1	1.1	.7	43	60	.7	13	244	1,900	.07	.13	.6	78
Cooked, boiled, drained	91.4	26	3.1	.2	4.7	1.1	.6	41	58	.7	12	220	1,900	.06	.11	.5	73
Brussels sprouts:																	
Raw	85.2	45	4.9	.4	8.3	1.6	1.2	36	80	1.5	14	390	550	.10	.16	.9	102
Cooked, boiled, drained	88.2	36	4.2	.4	6.4	1.6	.8	32	72	1.1	10	273	520	.08	.14	.8	87
Frozen:																	
Not thawed:	88.4	36	3.3	.2	7.3	1.2	.8	22	62	.9	16	328	570	.10	.11	.6	87
Cooked, boiled, drained	89.3	33	3.2	.2	6.5	1.2	.8	21	61	.8	14	295	570	.08	.10	.6	81
Cabbage:																	
Common varieties (Danish, domestic, and pointed types:																	
Raw	92.4	24	1.3	.2	5.4	.8	.7	49	29	.4	20	233	130	.05	.05	.3	47
Cooked, boiled until tender, drained:																	
Shredded, cooked in small amount of water	93.9	20	1.1	.2	4.3	.8	.5	44	20	.3	14	163	130	.04	.04	.3	33
Wedges, cooked in large amount of water	94.3	18	1.0	.2	4.0	.8	.5	42	17	.3	13	151	120	.02	.02	.1	24

COMPOSITION OF FOODS (continued)

Food and Description	Water	Food energy	Protein	Fat	Carbohydrate		Ash	Calcium	Phosphorus	Iron	Sodium	Potassium	Vitamin A value	Thiamine	Riboflavin	Niacin	Ascorbic acid
					Total	Fiber											
	Percent	Calories	Grams	Grams	Grams	Grams	Grams	Milligrams	Milligrams	Milligrams	Milligrams	Milligrams	International unit	Milligrams	Milligrams	Milligrams	Milligrams
Dehydrated	4	308	12.4	1.7	73.7	10.3	8.2	405	287	3.9	190	2,207	1,300	.45	.40	3.0	211
Red, raw	90.2	31	2.0	.2	6.9	1.0	.7	42	35	.8	26	268	40	.09	.06	.4	61
Savoy, raw	92.0	24	2.4	.2	4.6	.8	.8	67	54	.9	22	269	200	.05	.08	.3	55
Cauliflower:																	
Raw	91.0	27	2.7	.2	5.2	1.0	.9	25	56	1.1	13	295	60	.11	.10	.7	78
Cooked, boiled, drained	92.8	22	2.3	.2	4.1	1.0	.6	21	42	.7	9	206	60	.09	.08	.6	55
Frozen:																	
Not thawed:	92.9	22	2.0	.2	4.3	.8	.6	19	42	.6	11	225	30	.06	.06	.5	56
Cooked, boiled, drained	94.0	18	1.9	.2	3.3	.8	.6	17	38	.5	10	207	30	.04	.05	.4	41
Collards:																	
Raw:																	
Leaves, without stems	85.3	45	4.8	0.8	7.5	1.2	1.6	250	82	1.5	—	450	9,300	0.16	0.31	1.7	152
Leaves, including stems	86.9	40	3.6	.7	7.2	.9	1.6	203	63	1.0	43	401	6,500	.20	(.31)	(1.7)	92
Cooked, boiled, drained																	
Leaves without stems, cooked in —																	
Small amount of water	89.6	33	3.6	.7	5.1	1.0	1.0	188	52	.8	—	262	7,800	.11	.20	1.2	76
Large amount of water	90.2	31	3.4	.7	4.8	1.0	.9	177	48	.8	—	243	7,800	.07	.14	1.1	51
Leaves including stems, cooked in —																	
Small amount of water	90.8	29	2.7	.6	4.9	.8	1.0	152	39	.6	25	234	5,400	.14	.20	1.2	46
Frozen:																	
Not thawed	89.7	32	3.1	.4	5.8	1.0	1.0	191	53	1.1	18	259	6,800	.07	.16	.7	68
Cooked, boiled, drained	90.2	30	2.9	.4	5.6	1.0	.9	176	51	1.0	16	236	6,800	.06	.14	.6	33
Kale:																	
Raw:																	
Leaves, without stems, midribs	82.7	53	(6.0)	(.8)	9.0	—	(1.5)	249	93	2.7	(75)	(378)	10,000	.16	.26	2.1	186
Leaves, including stems	87.5	38	4.2	.8	6.0	1.3	1.5	179	73	2.2	75	378	8,900	—	—	—	125
Cooked, boiled, drained																	
Leaves, without stems, midribs	87.8	39	(4.5)	(.7)	6.1	—	(.9)	187	58	1.6	(43)	(221)	8,300	.10	.18	1.6	93
Leaves, including stems	91.2	28	3.2	.7	4.0	1.1	.9	134	46	1.2	43	221	7,400	—	—	—	62

COMPOSITION OF FOODS (continued)

Food and Description	Water	Food energy	Pro-tein	Fat	Carbohydrate Total	Carbohydrate Fiber	Ash	Cal-cium	Phos-phorus	Iron	Sod-ium	Potas-sium	Vitamin A units	Thia-mine	Ribo-flavin	Niacin	Ascor-bic acid
	Percent	Calories	Grams	Grams	Grams	Grams	Grams	Milli-grams	Milli-grams	Milli-grams	Milli-grams	Milli-grams	Inter-national value	Milli-grams	Milli-grams	Milli-grams	Milli-grams
Frozen:																	
Not thawed	90.0	32	3.2	.5	5.5	.9	.8	134	50	1.1	26	241	8,200	.08	.18	.8	64
Cooked, boiled, drained	90.5	31	3.0	.5	5.4	.9	.6	121	48	1.0	21	193	8,200	.06	.15	.7	38
Kohlrabi, thickened bulb-like stems:																	
Raw	90.3	29	2.0	.1	6.6	1.0	1.0	41	51	.5	8	372	20	.06	.04	.3	66
Cooked, boiled, drained	92.2	24	1.7	.1	5.3	1.0	.7	33	41	.3	6	260	20	.06	.03	.2	43
Mustard greens:																	
Raw	89.5	31	3.0	.5	5.6	1.1	1.4	183	50	3.0	32	377	7,000	.11	.22	.8	97
Cooked, boiled, drained .	92.6	23	2.2	.4	4.0	.9	.8	138	32	1.8	18	220	5,800	.08	.14	.6	48
Frozen:																	
Not thawed	93.5	20	2.3	.4	3.2	1.0	.6	115	45	1.6	12	196	6,000	.04	.12	.4	34
Cooked, boiled, drained .	93.8	20	2.2	.4	3.1	1.0	.5	104	43	1.5	10	157	6,000	.03	.10	.4	20
Rutabagas:																	
Raw	87.0	46	1.1	.1	11.0	1.1	.8	66	39	.4	5	239	580	.07	.07	1.1	43
Cooked, boiled, drained .	90.2	35	.9	.1	8.2	1.1	.6	59	31	.3	4	167	550	.06	.06	.8	26
Sauerkraut, canned, solids and liquid	92.8	18	1.0	.2	4.0	.7	2.0	36	18	.5	747	140	50	.03	.04	.2	14
Sauerkraut juice, canned	94.6	10	.7	Trace	2.3	Trace	2.4	37	14	1.1	787	—	—	.03	.04	.2	18
Turnips:																	
Raw	91.5	30	1.0	.2	6.6	.9	.7	39	30	.5	49	268	Trace	.04	.07	.6	26
Cooked, boiled, drained	93.6	23	.8	.2	4.9	.9	.5	35	24	.4	34	188	Trace	.04	.05	.3	22
Turnip greens, leaves including stems:																	
Raw	90.3	28	3.0	.3	5.0	.8	1.4	246	58	1.8	—	—	7,600	(.21)	(.39)	(.8)	139
Cooked, boiled, drained, cooked in —																	
Small amount of water, short time	93.2	20	2.2	.2	3.6	.7	.8	184	37	1.1	—	—	6,300	.15	.24	.6	69
Large amount of water, long time	93.5	19	2.2	.2	3.3	.7	.8	174	34	1.0	—	—	5,700	.10	.23	.5	47
Canned, solids and liquid	93.7	18	1.5	0.3	3.2	0.7	1.3	100	30	1.6	236	243	4,700	0.02	0.09	0.6	19
Frozen:																	
Not thawed	92.3	23	2.6	.3	4.0	1.0	.8	131	41	1.7	23	188	6,900	.06	.11	.5	34
Cooked, boiled, drained	92.7	23	2.5	.3	3.9	1.0	.6	118	39	1.6	17	149	6,900	.05	.09	.4	19

*Excerpted from Nutritive Value of Foods, USDA, Home & Garden Bulletin No. 72.

FACTS & FIGURES

*It was as true . . . as turnips is. It was as true . . . as taxes is.
And nothing's truer than them.*

—Charles Dickens

HORTICULTURALISTS CLASSIFY CRUCIFEROUS plants by the parts used for food—leaves, flowers, stems, or roots—and by the ways in which those parts develop: the loose, open leaves of collards, kale, mustard, and turnip greens; the heads of Brussels sprouts and cabbage formed by closely wrapped leaves; both stems and buds of broccoli and cauliflower; the aboveground tuber of kohlrabi; and the below-ground bulbs of rutabagas and turnips.

Most Broccoli & Company vegetables grow and mature best in moderate-to-cool temperatures, though some, like broccoli, originated and are widely cultivated in the sea-warmed areas near the Mediterranean.

In some regions of North Africa, certain wild cruciferous plants make up a major part of the vegetation. Thousands of varieties are considered inedible weeds even though many are rich in important vitamin C. Only a few varieties have assumed starring roles as food crops.

Cabbage has traditionally occupied the *Dai Ichi* or Number One position in the *BROCCOLI & COMPANY* family of vegetables, but broccoli is threatening that rating, at least in the United States where it was introduced as a commercial crop in the 1920s. Marketed to families of Italian extraction, largely on the east and west coasts, its popularity quickly spread, and it became an important truck garden crop in the vast agricultural valleys of California.

By the early 1950s, United States broccoli production was over 150 million pounds: It more than doubled that by 1965. Since then, production has skyrocketed as growers have attempted to keep up with an astonishing 767 percent increase in consumption. The number of farms producing broccoli has increased at an annual rate of 14 percent since 1978.

There are two types of broccoli—heading and sprouting. Both are classified by botanists as members of genus *Brassica*, though of different groups. Heading broccoli is, in effect, a slow-growing, winter-type of cauliflower. It looks for all the world like cauliflower but is difficult to grow and is not widely marketed in the United States. Sprouting broccoli is the familiar, bright green plant commonly grown and marketed in the United States and Europe as broccoli. It forms a loose flower head on a tall, green, fleshy branching stalk instead of the compact head or curd found on cauliflower and heading broccoli.

About 90 percent of the fresh broccoli in the United States is grown in California. Other growing areas include Oregon, Colorado, Texas, Ohio, and Florida. Most of what they produce is marketed fresh or frozen. In California, where it is harvested from February through December, broccoli yields can be as high as 8000 pounds per acre.

One cup of cooked broccoli contains only 40 calories; about 68 percent of the safe form of vitamin A (beta-carotene) recommended daily for an average adult; and more than twice the daily allowance of vitamin C. It is also rich in minerals.

An average serving (half cup) of broccoli contains 7 grams of carbohydrates, more crude fiber than the same amount of celery, and significant amounts of vitamins E, B_1, B_2, and B_6, along with 4 percent of the daily iron and calcium requirements for an average adult. It has 480 mg of potassium, and measurable amounts of magnesium, niacin, phosphorus, copper, zinc, and pantothenic acid; 4-5 grams of protein, only 1-2 grams of fat, and *no* cholesterol.

Brussels sprouts are a good source of protein, iron, calcium, phosphorus, potassium, and vitamins A, B, and C. One cup of cooked Brussels sprouts has 160 percent of the recommended daily allowance of vitamin C, 10 percent of the thiamine, 10+ percent of the iron; but fewer than 50 calories.

Cabbage, which got its name when the French word for pate—*caboche*—was Anglicized to *cabbage*, has ruled as king of cruciferous vegetables throughout the centuries. Some believe cabbage was first cultivated in the Orient more than 4000 years ago. Others say evidence points to cabbages having first appeared in Asia Minor, developing from a wild, leafy plant that grew without producing a head.

The ancient Romans are credited by some authorities with introducing cabbage into Europe after finding it growing in the gardens of people they conquered in the Near East. It was prized not only for its nutrition, but also for its medicinal effects.

Others say that cabbage was patiently developed from wild or "sea" cabbages in prehistoric times by Europeans and/or the English. Descendants of those wild cabbages still grow along lonely English seacoasts and other desolate places around the world, but they bear little resemblance to domesticated varieties. The wild plants grow up to two feet high, with smooth leaves and large yellow flowers, but no heads. Yet the seeds, seed pods, and flowers of the cabbages we grow in our gardens and buy in our supermarkets are still essentially the same as those of their wild cousins and distant ancestors.

From earliest times, the cabbage has been appreciated for its ability to handle the cold winter climates of Europe and Asia, even as far north as Lapland and Siberia. It continues to grow and stay fresh in field and garden well into the fall; after harvesting it can be stored to provide fresh nutrition far into the winter. Slavs, Germans, and Scandinavians also learned to preserve it as sauerkraut, thus stretching its "shelf-life." Cabbage is still eastern Europe's most important vegetable. Annual average consumption in the Soviet Union, for example, is 66 pounds per person, more than 30 percent of all vegetables eaten. That compares with 10–12 pounds for the average American, or about 6 percent of our vegetable diet.

Cabbage was first introduced into North America by the French navigator, Jacques Cartier, in 1541. Both early European settlers and Native American Indians planted it, and it spread across the continent with the pioneers. Today it is widely cultivated in the United States. Among the major commercial production centers are California, Texas, New Jersey, New York, North Carolina, Ohio, Virginia, and Wisconsin. Production totals several billion pounds annually.

Cabbage is rich in ascorbic acid (vitamin C) and it retains high amounts of the vitamin even after weeks of cold storage. A wedge 3 ½ by 4 ½ inches has over 80 percent of the vitamin C needed daily by an average adult, along with beta-carotene (the safe form of vitamin A), fiber, thiamine, iron, folic acid, carbohydrates, calcium, and other minerals; but fewer than 30 calories.

Though California produces more cauliflower than any other state, it is produced also in Michigan, Arizona, New York, Texas, and Oregon, including a purple variety that turns green when cooked, and tastes like broccoli.

A cup of raw cauliflower has more than the recommended daily allowance of vitamin C for an average adult. A cup cooked, with fewer than 50 calories, has 80 percent of the RDA of vitamin C, in addition to protein, carbohydrates, fiber, calcium, iron, and other minerals and vitamins.

Greens are noted for the nutrients they add to our diets. The leafy portions contain more nutrients than the stems and midribs and are excellent sources of beta-carotene, vitamin C, calcium, and fiber. There are fewer than 30 calories per half-cup serving.

Collards—called nonheading or tree cabbage—got its name from the Anglo-Saxon "colewyrts," meaning "cabbage plants." It is believed to have been grown for food in Asia Minor for several millennia. The plants form large rosettes of coarse leaves instead of heads, on tall, thick stems.

An average serving (half cup) of cooked collards with only 21 calories provides 87 percent of the vitamin A (in the safe form of beta-carotene), 74 percent of the vitamin C, and 14 percent of the calcium in the minimum daily requirements of an average adult. They are also a good source of folic acid, iron, and thiamine.

Kale has been grown for food at least since 200 B.C. A native of Europe, it is prized for its succulent leaves and stems. One serving (half cup) cooked provides an average adult with daily requirements of vitamin C and vitamin A (in the safe form of beta-carotene), and 13 percent of the calcium requirements, yet it has only 21 calories.

Kohlrabi, characterized by a bulb that grows above ground, has been in use as a food plant in Europe since the sixteenth century, and in the United States since the early 1800s. Kohlrabi bulbs can be either light green or pale violet in color. They are a good source of beta-carotene, vitamin C, calcium, phosphorous, iron, and some of the B-complex vitamins.

One serving (half cup) of raw kohlrabi has 147 percent of the recommended daily allowance of vitamin C for average adults, several minerals, and fiber. One serving cooked has 91 percent of the RDA of vitamin C.

Mustard, also known as "mustard greens," is grown for its tender leaves and stems. The plant originated in China and Asia and is different from the species which produces seed used in making table mustard. One research study into the production of nutrients per acre of different crops showed mustard greens ranking highest, with broccoli and turnips close behind.

One cup of cooked mustard greens has only 23 calories, but it provides *61 percent more than* the recommended daily allowance of vitamin A (as safe beta-carotene) for an average adult; *more than* the total allowance of vitamin C (as ascorbic acid); 20 percent of the iron; and more than 12 percent of the calcium required daily by an average adult.

A half-cup serving of rutabagas has about 35 calories, 9 grams of protein, 8 grams of carbohydrates, 1 gram of fiber, 59 mg of calcium, 31 mg of phosphorus, 3 mg of iron, 167 mg of potassium, 330 IU of beta-carotene (the safe form of vitamin A), 26 mg of ascorbic acid (vitamin C), and small amounts of thiamine, riboflavin, and niacin.

A medium turnip contains more than half the recommended daily allowance for average adults of vitamin C, yet a half-cup serving has fewer than 35 calories.

A certain professor came to visit a colleague, who happened to be away. The guest was greeted by the absentee's eccentric sisters. They were friendly and solicitous, and the professor stayed for dinner. "What will you have?" the three sisters entreated anxiously. "Oh, the best you've got," replied the professor, smiling. So they stewed the family Bible with the cabbage.

—Annie Fields

BUY TOP QUALITY cruciferous vegetables, at their best for eating fresh, as if you had grown them in your own garden: in season, mature, well-colored, and free of bruises, skin punctures, and decay. (See information relating to specific varieties, below.) Buy only as much as you need, either for use immediately or for short- or long-term storage. Discard parts that show signs of decay. Do not wash until ready to use.

For short-term storage, place different kinds of vegetables in separate plastic bags or in separate crisper drawers in the refrigerator. Set the refrigerator at 32°-41° F. and maintain relative humidity of between 85-95 percent by keeping plastic bags or crisper drawers more than half full. (See page 14 for refrigerator storage times.)

For long-term storage, either can, dry, or freeze, following directions supplied by manufacturers of equipment used for such purposes.

Should you have the facilities and the desire for storing *cruciferae* in basements, cellars, outbuildings, and pits, detailed instructions for doing so can be found in Home and Garden Bulletin No. 119, available from the U.S. Department of Agriculture, Washington, D.C. 20250.

BROCCOLI

Look for bud clusters that are firm and compact, with color ranging from sage green to dark green to purplish green. Stems should be 8-10 inches long, neither thick nor tough. Avoid bunches with spread bud clusters, watersoaked spots, enlarged or open buds, yellowish green color, or wilted condition.

BRUSSELS SPROUTS

Look for fresh, bright green color, tight-fitting outer leaves, firm body, and small size. Avoid sprouts with yellow or yellowish green leaves which have holes, and ragged or loose leaves that are soft or wilted.

CABBAGE

Look for firm or hard heads that are solid and heavy for their size. Outer leaves should be a good green or red color, reasonably fresh, and free from serious blemishes. Some early-crop cabbage may be soft or only fairly firm, but can be used in a timely fashion if crisp and fresh. Avoid cabbage with yellow, wilted, worm-eaten, or decayed outer leaves, or leaf stems separated from the central base.

CAULIFLOWER

Look for heads with stark or creamy white compact, solid, and clean curd. Avoid wilted heads with curd that is spread apart, smudgy, discolored, or speckled.

GREENS (collards, kale, mustard, and turnip)

Look for fresh, young, tender leaves that are free from blemishes and a bright healthy green color. Avoid leaves with coarse, fibrous stems, yellowish green color, softness, a wilted condition, or evidence of insects, such as aphids.

KOHLRABI

Look for round small-to-medium size bulbs no more than 2-3 inches in diameter that are firm and crisp, with lively green tops. Avoid limp, discolored bulbs with deep punctures or signs of decay.

RUTABAGA and TURNIP

Look for small-to-medium size bulbs that are smooth, fairly round and firm, heavy for their size. Avoid large bulbs with too many leaf scars around the top, obvious fibrous roots, skin punctures, deep cuts, or decay.

SHORT- AND LONG-TERM STORAGE

Variety	Store in Refrigerator (Weeks)	Long-Term Storage
Broccoli	1-2	Can/Dry/Freeze
Brussels Sprouts	3-4	Can/Dry/Freeze
Cabbage	12-16	Can/Dry/Freeze
Cauliflower	2-3	Can/Dry/Freeze
Collards	1-2	Can/Dry/Freeze
Kale	1-2	Can/Dry/Freeze
Kohlrabi	2-4	Can/Dry/Freeze
Mustard Greens	1-2	Can/Dry/Freeze
Rutabaga	8-16	Can/Dry/Freeze
Turnip Greens	1-2	Can/Dry/Freeze
Turnips	8-12	Can/Dry/Freeze

*Training is everything. The peach was once a bitter almond;
cauliflower is nothing but cabbage with a college education.*

—Mark Twain

USE BROCCOLI & COMPANY vegetables as soon as possible after picking or purchasing fresh to get maximum benefit from the vitamins and minerals they contain. When ready to use, wash carefully, avoid soaking, and peel, cut, chop, dice, mince, or shred at the last minute to reduce nutrient loss.

Conserve vitamin C content by storing in a cold or cool place and by not peeling or slicing until just before use. Vitamin C and some other vitamins are destroyed by contact with oxygen, which is kept out by vegetable skin. The less surface exposed to oxygen, the less vitamin loss.

Cruciferous vegetables have elements that make them colorful as well as nutritious: the green of chlorophyll, the red of anthocyanin, and the ivory of flavone. Minimal cooking in a minimum of water brings out the best in both color and flavor. Save cooking water with its nutrients and add to soup stocks, broths, and tonics.

The most healthful methods of cooking include baking, roasting, oven-broiling, microwave cooking, boiling, steaming, poaching, stir-frying, and stewing. Avoid barbecuing, grilling, or smoking. Leave uncovered for the first 5 minutes of cooking, cover, and continue cooking 10-15 minutes, or until crisp-tender. Or cook covered, lifting the lid several times to permit escape of gases which may dull the color of the vegetables and give them a strong taste.

While cooking tends to destroy some of the water-soluble vitamin C found in Broccoli & Company vegetables, the fat-soluble beta-carotene they contain is not significantly or adversely affected by heat.

Nutritionists recommend cooking in stainless steel, enamel, or glass pans. *Never* cook in pans made of aluminum or copper which react with sulfur compounds in the vegetables to create unpleasant odors and flavors, and destroy vitamin C, folic acid, and vitamin E.

The cooking process helps to break down cellulose in Broccoli & Company vegetables, making it easier for our systems to assimilate the beta-carotene (provitamin A) they contain.

In most of the recipes calling for oil, we have specified canola oil, which is produced in Canada (hence, *canola*) by pressing the seeds of the rape plant, a member of the cruciferous family. Canola oil has no cholesterol, and less saturated fat than any other vegetable oil, including safflower, sunflower, corn, soybean, peanut, and olive oils. In important monounsaturated fat content, canola is second only to olive oil. Canola oil is odorless and has no discernible taste to compete with the delicate flavors of *cruciferae*, whether raw or cooked. If not available, one can use any light, low cholesterol oil.

Mindful of the dangers to health that are inherent in cholesterol, dairy fats, animal fats, and saturated vegetable fats, we have specified soft margarine, low-fat milk, low-fat yogurt, and low-fat cheese in most recipes that call for margarine, milk, yogurt, or cheese.

We advise against the addition of soda, lemon juice, or any other ingredient except the barest minimum of salt to water in which vegetables are cooked. Though such additions may shorten cooking time and enhance color and whiteness, they may have a detrimental effect on the texture, and the vitamin and mineral content of the superior vegetables that are included in *BROCCOLI & COMPANY*.

Broccoli. Fresh young broccoli is delicious in salads and on platters of raw vegetables. To prepare, wash and shake dry. Remove florets and set aside. Peel the stalk if necessary to remove tough fibers, cut in half lengthwise, and julienne. Serve reserved florets and julienned strips with a variety of dressings, sauces, and dips. A pound is enough to provide 3-4 servings of medium size.

Broccoli can be cooked to tender crispness and flavored with a little soft margarine or butter; stir-fried with lean meat and Oriental sauces; pureed for soups or soufflés; and added to omelettes or quiches.

Brief cooking brightens the deep bluish green color and the unique flavor of broccoli, while prolonged cooking dulls both color and taste. Prepare stems and florets as directed above, then make lengthwise cuts almost to the crown in stems more than ½ inch in diameter, so they will cook as quickly as the florets. When using only the florets, reserve stems for use in soups, sauces, salads, or other dishes.

Cook whole broccoli stalks loose in a covered saucepan with 1 inch of boiling water and salt to taste. Leave uncovered for the first 5 minutes, cover, and cook 10-15 minutes, or just until crisp-tender in order to preserve nutrients such as vitamin C. To cook upright, tie stems together in a bunch and stand in a deep pan. Do not overcook. Accent the flavor by sprinkling with such combinations as melted soft margarine, fine dry bread crumbs, and salt and pepper to taste.

Combine cooked broccoli with a cheese or sour cream sauce and serve on toast, pasta, or mashed potatoes; add leftover pieces to soups, spaghetti sauce, and scrambled eggs.

Brussels sprouts. Brussels sprouts are just coming to harvest when hot weather greens are fading. Wash, trim, and quarter the sprouts, toss with *Celery Seed Dressing* (see page 52), and sprinkle with Parmesan cheese and minced hard-cooked eggs. Thinly sliced, they can substitute for cabbage in coleslaw and other salad recipes (see pages 48, 52, and 55). One pound is enough for 4 half-cup servings.

Combine thinly sliced raw Brussels sprouts with English walnut halves on a bed of crisp salad greens, and serve with *Yogurt Dressing* (see page 54).

When preparing Brussels sprouts for cooking, trim stem ends and cut crosses into the bases to reduce cooking time. Cook without a cover in a minimum amount of water for about 5 minutes; cover and cook 10-15 minutes longer, or until crisp-tender.

Toss cooked Brussels sprouts with melted soft margarine combined with tarragon or sweet basil, slivered almonds, chopped pecans, English walnuts, or croutons; or sour cream blended with minced parsley and a dash of lemon juice.

Sprinkle cooked Brussels sprouts with nutmeg, sage, or caraway; or combine with thin slices of crisp raw kohlrabi or water chestnuts. Serve steamed sprouts with baked sweet potatoes and sautéed mushrooms.

Cabbage. One pound of cabbage is enough to make 5-6 cups minced, 4-5 cups sliced, and 4-4 ½ cups shredded. Vitamin C loss can be minimized by using a knife rather than a chopper, and then using the cabbage as soon as possible.

In addition to use as a salad, coleslaw can be added to any meat sandwich in place of—or in addition to—lettuce.

Prepare cabbage for cooking by trimming the base and removing torn or discolored outer leaves. Cut into quarters and remove the wedge of core from each. Slice or shred with a long slicing knife or in a food processor. Cut vitamin loss by cooking uncovered for 5 minutes in a minimum of water, and then for 10 minutes, or until crisp-tender.

Sprinkle a few leaves of savory in the water in which you steam or boil cabbage wedges. Cook until nearly done, then stir in a dash of curry powder and a pat of soft margarine. Cook until crisp-tender, and serve, dotted with more margarine and salt and pepper to taste.

Cauliflower. A medium head of cauliflower weighing about 1 pound will yield some 3 cups of florets, or enough to serve 4-6 people.

Serve raw cauliflowerets with dips and sauces: Choose the whitest head of cauliflower you can find, wash well, and scrape off any spots with the edge of a sharp knife. Cut florets away from the core and arrange on a platter or tray with other crudités and dips. Reserve the core for use in soups and mixed vegetable dishes.

Cauliflower can be boiled, blanched, steamed, braised, sautéed, stir-fried, deep-fried, or microwaved. To cook whole, bring 1 inch of water to a boil, add the head of cauliflower, and cook 5 minutes uncovered. Cover and cook 15-25 minutes, or until crisp-tender.

To use cauliflowerets only, cut floret stems loose from the core, or rotate a large knife around the core and remove. Reserve the core for use in soups, salads, sauces, egg or mixed vegetable dishes.

Enhance cauliflower by serving with a variety of sauces: Heat leftover *Chili con Carrot* (see page 85 in *THE CARROT COOKBOOK*, Garden Way Publishing) or spaghetti sauce and serve over a cooked whole cauliflower; mix 1 cup of sour cream and 4 tablespoons chopped English walnuts to go with cooked, hot cauliflowerets; or melt 3 tablespoons soft margarine, whisk in 1 teaspoon of lemon juice and a dash of chervil, and serve over steaming cauliflowerets.

Greens. Collard greens, kale, mustard greens, young kohlrabi leaves, and turnip greens are made of sterner stuff than spinach and swiss chard. They should be prepared for cooking by removing and discarding heavy stalks and center veins. Shred leaves across the veins, and tear or slice into pieces of desired size. One pound trimmed is enough for about 4 half-cup servings.

To cook collards, place in a minimum of water in a saucepan, cook uncovered 5 minutes, cover, and simmer 10-15 minutes, or until tender, stirring occasionally. Or cook covered, lifting the lid often to permit gases to escape. Serve greens with cooking liquid, which is full of nutrients. For a Southern flavor in greens, sauté a small amount of bacon or salt pork until crisp; drain, add to the greens, and cook, following directions above.

Make a cream sauce for greens by stirring 2 tablespoons all-purpose flour into 2 tablespoons canola oil in a medium saucepan. When bubbly, add 1 ½ cups low-fat milk, and salt and pepper to taste. Stir until smooth and thick. Serve over cooked collards, kale, kohlrabi, mustard, or turnip greens. Sprinkle with grated low-fat cheese.

Ruffles of deep red and green raw kale can be torn into bite-size pieces to accent salads and relish trays; or cook in a small amount of water, mix into tossed salads to add body and nutrients; or serve as a side dish with a sprinkle of lemon juice and a dab or two of soft margarine.

Most Broccoli & Company greens have a slight bluish tint, but some mustard leaves look bronze and some are light green: Both variations are normal. When young and tender, greens can be used raw in salads: Older leaves should be cooked for serving as a side dish, or added to soups and stews to provide flavor, color, and nutrients.

To cook mustard greens, place in a small amount of water in a covered pan and boil 15-20 minutes, or until tender. Lift the lid of the pan several times to release gases that may cause the greens to discolor and have a strong taste.

Kohlrabi. Kohlrabi, the "aboveground turnip," which is a cross between a turnip and a cabbage, has a taste similar to that of young sweet turnips and cabbages. Tender small bulbs can be steamed with the skin on and served hot, or cooled, diced, and added to salads.

Older kohlrabi bulbs have thick fibrous skin and should be peeled just before use by stripping off the skin with a sharp knife. Cut out all of the tough, inedible fibrous base. Quarter or slice and boil in as little salted water as possible for 25-35 minutes, or until tender, lifting the lid from time to time to allow gases to escape.

Crisp and crunchy thin slices of raw kohlrabi can be added to dishes in place of water chestnuts. They can also be julienned and served on trays of relishes and crudités.

To cook tender young kohlrabi bulbs, wash and boil unpeeled in a small amount of lightly salted water until crisp-tender. Serve hot with flavorings and sea-sonings such as lemon juice, chives, melted soft margarine, and grated cheese to taste.

Prepare stuffed kohlrabi by cooking the bulbs, scooping out the centers, dicing, and combining with sautéed onion and ground meat. Spoon the meat mixture into the kohlrabi shells and bake at 375° F. for 15-20 minutes, or until piping hot and golden brown.

Rutabaga. A medium rutabaga yields 1 cup diced and cooked. A pound provides 4 half-cup servings.

Prepare rutabagas for cooking by cutting off leaves and stem ends, and paring off the thick skin of older bulbs. Leave skin on young tender bulbs unless they have been waxed for storage at your supermarket. Slice, quarter, dice, or julienne, and cook covered in as little boiling water as possible for 15-25 minutes, or until tender. Lift the lid from time to time to allow gases to escape.

Rutabagas may also be boiled or baked in their skins; boiled and mashed; cooked, diced, and combined with other vegetables such as carrots and celery; cooked, diced, and added to potato salad; julienned and French fried; or sliced paper-thin and cottage fried with thin slices of sweet onion.

For a special treat, sprinkle cooked cubes of rutabaga with sugar, molasses, and salt to taste. Sauté in melted soft margarine until golden brown and crispy.

Turnip. When diced and cooked, a medium turnip will yield 1 cup. A pound provides 4 half-cup servings.

Snowy white or pale yellow raw turnips taste sweet because of their high sugar content. Cooking converts that sugar to starch. To serve raw, peel, slice, and arrange on a platter with or without other crudités.

Prepare turnips for cooking by cutting off leaves and stem ends, and paring off the thick skin of older bulbs. Leave skin on young tender bulbs. Slice, quarter, dice, or julienne. Place in a saucepan with a small amount of boiling water and cook uncovered for 5 minutes. Cover and continue cooking for 10-15 minutes, or until tender. Or cook covered, lifting the lid several times to allow gases to escape.

Turnips may be baked in their skins. Preheat the oven to 375° F., cut a cross in the side of each bulb to allow steam to escape, and bake for 25-45 minutes, or until tender. Serve with soft margarine and salt and pepper to taste.

Add cooked, diced turnips to stews and soups; mash and serve with soft margarine, salt, and pepper; combine with a mild cheese sauce; or flavor with lemon juice, soft margarine, pepper, and basil.

APPETIZERS & HORS D'OEUVRES

We may live without poetry, music, and art; we may live without conscience, and live without heart; we may live without friends; we may live without books; but civilized man cannot live without cooks.

—The Earl of Lytton

CRUDITÉS

PREPARATION TIME: VARIABLE
YIELD: VARIABLE

broccoli florets
cauliflowerets
cabbage
wooden toothpicks
turnips
kohlrabi
rutabaga

Broccoli florets and cauliflowerets are often featured raw on salad bars or served as hors d'oeuvres with dips of various kinds. Other members of BROCCOLI & COMPANY, such as cabbage, turnips, kohlrabi, and rutabaga, are familiar to many only when cooked. Knowing how much vitamin C they contain raw, we serve them often on relish trays and as hors d'oeuvres.

Wash and drain broccoli spears and cauliflower heads. Cut or snap the florets loose from the stems and arrange on relish tray or salad plate. Set aside.

Wash, halve, and quarter the cabbage, removing and discarding the core. Peel leaves from the quarters and roll into tubes, securing with wooden toothpicks. Arrange on relish tray or salad plate. Set aside.

Peel and julienne turnips, kohlrabi, and rutabaga. Arrange on relish tray or salad tray. Serve with reserved crudités, above, and a dip or fondue (see pages 23, 28).

BACON-WRAPPED BRUSSELS SPROUTS

PREPARATION TIME: 15-20 MINUTES
YIELD: VARIABLE

Brussels sprouts
bacon strips, extra lean and extra thin
wooden toothpicks

Cook the Brussels sprouts in as little water as possible, salted to taste. Drain and set aside.

Preheat the broiler and have the broiler tray ready.

Cut the bacon strips in two lengthwise and in half across their width. Wrap the strips around the reserved Brussels sprouts, securing ends with toothpicks.

Arrange the bacon-wrapped sprouts on the broiler tray and broil, turning once, until the bacon is well done and crisp.

Remove from the broiler and serve at once.

ROQUEFORT DIP

PREPARATION TIME: 10-15 MINUTES
YIELD: ABOUT 1¼ CUPS

½ cup plain low-fat yogurt
½ cup sour cream
1 teaspoon lemon juice
dash garlic powder
¼ cup Roquefort cheese, crumbled

We have given our formula for this simple, delicious dip, but it can be adjusted to suit your taste by altering proportions of yogurt, sour cream, and cheese.

In a small mixing bowl, blend the yogurt, the sour cream, the lemon juice, the garlic powder, and the cheese.

Turn into a dish and serve, or cover and chill until ready to use.

BOTANAS

PREPARATION TIME: 25-30 MINUTES
YIELD: 4-6 SERVINGS

We are very fond of the botanas served at a favorite Michigan restaurant, but we think our version is even better, with vitamin C and beta-carotene-rich broccoli and cauliflower bits added to the usual toppings.

4-6 cups refried beans
½-¾ cup tomato sauce
salt and pepper to taste
¼ teaspoon garlic powder,
    or to taste
16-20 ounces plain tortilla chips
2 cups grated low-fat cheese

Toppings:
1 cup thinly sliced broccoli florets
1 cup thinly sliced cauliflowerets
1 cup thinly sliced Spanish onion
1 cup thinly sliced green pepper
2 tomatoes, thinly sliced
2 avocados, thinly sliced
1 cup dill pickle chips
1 cup stuffed green olives,
    thinly sliced
1 cup pitted black olives,
    thinly sliced

Combine the beans, the tomato sauce, the salt and pepper, and the garlic powder in a large covered saucepan and cook over low heat for 15-20 minutes, stirring occasionally, until spreadable.

Preheat the oven to 350° F.

Spread the tortilla chips on a large ovenproof platter or 4-6 oven-proof plates.

Spread the bean mixture over the reserved tortilla chips, sprinkle with the cheese, and place in the oven for 10-15 minutes, or until the cheese is melted.

Remove from the oven and top with the broccoli florets, the cauliflowerets, the onion, the green pepper, the tomatoes, the avocados, the pickle chips, and the olives. Serve.

LORRAINE'S EGG ROLLS

PREPARATION TIME: 20-30 MINUTES
YIELD: VARIABLE

½ cup apricot jam
3 tablespoons soy sauce, divided
1 tablespoon cider vinegar
1 cup minced broccoli florets
1 quarter cabbage, minced
8-10 kale leaves, minced
2 green onions, minced
1 medium carrot, grated
2 ribs celery, minced
2 cups bean sprouts
2 tablespoons cornstarch
¼ cup water
1 package egg roll wrappers
canola oil

These appetizers feature broccoli, cabbage, and kale—three adaptable Broccoli & Company vegetables. They can be made ahead of time, frozen, and reheated in the oven or microwave just before serving.

Puree the jam in a blender or processor and combine with 1 tablespoon of the soy sauce and the vinegar in a small covered saucepan. Cook over medium heat, stirring constantly, for 5 minutes. Remove from the heat and set aside.

In a large mixing bowl, combine the broccoli, the cabbage, the kale, the onions, the carrot, the celery, the bean sprouts, and 2 tablespoons of the soy sauce. Mix well and set aside.

Blend the cornstarch and the water in a small bowl. Set aside.

Lightly moisten the edges of one egg roll wrapper at a time and place 2-3 tablespoons of the broccoli mixture in the center. Fold two sides toward the center to cover the broccoli mixture partially, then roll like a tube, starting at one of the open ends. Remoisten the end of the roll with the cornstarch mixture if necessary to seal. Set aside.

Fill and roll the remaining wrappers with the remaining broccoli mixture until used up.

Place enough oil for deep frying in a large, heavy saucepan or deep fryer and heat to medium-high.

Cook the egg rolls a few at a time in the preheated oil until golden brown on both sides. Remove, drain on paper towels, and set aside, keeping warm.

Serve with the reserved jam mixture on the side, or cool, place in airtight plastic bags or containers, and freeze. Reheat in the oven or microwave when ready to use.

HOT BRUSSELS SPROUTS BALLS

PREPARATION TIME: 15-20 MINUTES
BAKING TIME: 10-15 MINUTES
YIELD: VARIABLE

Brussels sprouts
dry bread crumbs
Parmesan cheese, grated
chives, finely minced
salt and pepper to taste
egg whites
cocktail picks
sour cream

These piping hot little wonders are always party time hits. They can be prepared ahead of time, stored covered in the refrigerator, then popped into the oven after guests have arrived.

Preheat the oven to 450° F. Oil a baking sheet. Cook the Brussels sprouts crisp-tender in salted water. Drain and set aside.

In a medium mixing bowl, combine the bread crumbs and the cheese in a ratio of two parts crumbs to one part cheese. Stir in the chives to your taste, along with the salt and pepper. Set aside.

In a small mixing bowl, whisk the egg whites. Dip the reserved sprouts in the egg whites, roll in the cheese mixture, and arrange on the reserved baking sheet.

Bake 10-15 minutes, or until golden brown, turning once. Serve at once with cocktail picks and sour cream for dipping.

QUICHELETTES

PREPARATION TIME: 15-20 MINUTES
BAKING TIME: 20-30 MINUTES
YIELD: 16 QUICHELETTES

pastry dough for 9-inch double crust pie
1 ½ cups low-fat milk
1 tablespoon soft margarine
¼ cup minced onions
4 ounces low-fat mozzarella cheese,
   grated
4 ounces mushroom pieces, chopped
1 ½ cups cooked chopped broccoli
   pieces
2 eggs
¼ teaspoon oregano
salt and pepper to taste

We're willing to bet that neither you nor any of your guests will be able to stop at "just one" of these tiny temptations. They can be made ahead of time, frozen, and reheated just before serving.

Line sixteen 1 ½-inch muffin tins with the pastry dough. Chill. Preheat the oven to 375° F.

Scald the milk in a medium saucepan and set aside.

Melt the margarine in a small frying pan and sauté the onions until limp. Set aside.

Divide the cheese, the mushrooms, the reserved onions, and the broccoli equally among the lined muffin tins. Set aside.

In a large mixing bowl, beat the eggs, the reserved milk, the oregano, and the salt and pepper. Pour equally over the mixture in the muffin tins.

Bake for 20-30 minutes, or until firm. Remove from the oven and let stand 10 minutes. Remove from the muffin tins and serve at once.

FRESH FOOD FONDUE

PREPARATION TIME: 10-15 MINUTES
YIELD: ABOUT 1 CUP

1 ½ tablespoons soft margarine
1 ½ tablespoons all-purpose flour
¾ cup low-fat milk
½ cup shredded low-fat cheese
1 ½ teaspoons grated lemon zest
1 ½ teaspoons lemon juice
salt and pepper to taste
broccoli, celery, cabbage, green
  pepper, cauliflowerets, turnips,
  carrots, rutabaga, Brussels sprouts,
  and kohlrabi

Melt the margarine in a medium saucepan over medium heat, stir in the flour, and cook until bubbly. Add the milk and cook until thick, stirring constantly to prevent lumps.

Remove from the heat, add the cheese, the lemon zest, and the juice. Stir until melted. Salt and pepper to taste.

Turn into a fondue pot and keep warm. Serve with a platter of raw vegetables.

BRUSSELS SPROUTS VERONICA

PREPARATION TIME: 10-15 MINUTES
YIELD: 8-12 SERVINGS

Appetizers were probably developed not only to stimulate appetites and get digestive juices flowing, but also to ''tide over'' hungry dinner guests waiting for a meal to be served. We invented this particular variation for other reasons as well. It's delicious, it's low in calories, it's high in nutrition, it's easy to prepare, and it's delicious. Reasons enough.

2 tablespoons soft margarine or butter
3 cups cooked Brussels sprouts
1 ½ cups seedless red grapes
cocktail picks

Melt the margarine or butter over medium heat in a large frying pan. Add the Brussels sprouts and the grapes. Shake and stir until heated through.

Turn onto a platter and serve, with cocktail picks on the side.

RED CABBAGE ROLL-UPS

PREPARATION TIME: 10-15 MINUTES
YIELD: VARIABLE

Some people find it hard to believe that cabbage can be served raw in anything but coleslaw, but we've been making these colorful hors d'oeuvres from bright red cabbage leaves for some time now, and we've never had to deal with leftovers.

red cabbage
cream cheese, softened
bleu cheese
sour cream

Carefully peel the leaves from the cabbage. Cut in two, removing and reserving center spines.

Spread leaf halves with softened cream cheese or with bleu cheese and sour cream mixed until spreadable. Roll into tubes and cut in 2-inch lengths. Serve.

Use reserved leaf spines in *Viennese Red Cabbage* or *Stop-and-Go Salad* (see pages 75, 52).

SPROUTS AND CHESTNUTS EN BROCHETTE

PREPARATION TIME: 10-15 MINUTES
YIELD: 8-12 SERVINGS

2 cups cooked chestnuts
3 cups cooked Brussels sprouts
wooden cocktail skewers
2 tablespoons soft margarine or butter
salt and pepper

For variation, serve small containers of melted margarine or butter on the side, instead of adding before serving.

Preheat the oven to 300° F. Have ready an ovenproof serving platter.

Spear a chestnut and a sprout on each of the skewers, arrange on the platter and place in the oven for 10-15 minutes, or until warm.

Melt the margarine or butter in a small pan and dribble over the warmed chestnuts and sprouts, or serve on the side in individual dishes.

Serve immediately, with salt and pepper on the side.

SOUPS & PUREES

Soup of the evening, beautiful soup . . .
Who, for such dainties, would not stoop?
Soup of the evening, beautiful soup.

—Lewis Carroll

POTAGE DE NAVET

PREPARATION TIME: 30-45 MINUTES
YIELD: 4-6 SERVINGS

2 cups peeled diced turnips
1 medium potato, peeled and diced
1 small onion, minced
2 ½ cups chicken broth
¾-1 cup milk
salt and pepper to taste
croutons or nutmeg

This understated, elegant soup (made from turnips!*) is equally good whether served piping hot with crisp croutons, or dusted with nutmeg and refreshingly cold.*

Cook the turnips, the potato, and the onion in the chicken broth in a large saucepan for 20 minutes, or until tender.

Allow to cool slightly, then puree in a blender or processor.

Return the puree to the saucepan, add ¾ cup of milk, and salt and pepper to taste. Add the rest of the milk if too thick.

To serve hot, bring to just under a boil, remove from the heat, and ladle into a tureen. Float a handful of crisp croutons on the surface.

For cold soup, cool to room temperature, cover, and chill at least 4 hours. Dust a little nutmeg over the surface as you serve.

SATURDAY SOUP

PREPARATION TIME: 15-20 MINUTES
COOKING TIME: ABOUT 2 HOURS
YIELD: 6-8 SERVINGS

½-¾ **pound extra-lean beef stew**
  meat, diced
8-10 cups water
¼ **cup raw barley**
1 small onion, minced
2 medium carrots, coined
1 stalk celery, diced
1 medium kohlrabi, diced
1 medium potato, diced
½ **cup green lima beans**
¼ **teaspoon marjoram**
¼ **teaspoon ground sage**
beef broth
4 large leaves kale, chopped
1 tablespoon minced parsley
salt and pepper to taste

Soup on Saturday can get to be part of the weekend ritual, ranking right alongside Friday night popcorn and Sunday morning waffles as traditional fare. Once you've started the soup, you can let it simmer, smelling better and better as it cooks. At supper time, set out a basket of fresh yeast rolls and a tossed salad with the soup for one of the best meals of the week.

Place a large covered saucepan over medium-high heat and when a drop of water dances on the surface, sear the meat on all sides.

Reduce the heat to low and add 8 cups of water. Stir in the barley, the onion, the carrots, the celery, the kohlrabi, the potato, and the lima beans, along with the marjoram and the sage. Simmer covered for about 2 hours, adding beef broth if needed.

About 30 minutes before you are ready to serve the soup, add the kale, the parsley, and the salt and pepper.

Let simmer until ready. Ladle into a tureen or individual bowls and serve, with yeast rolls and tossed salad on the side.

PUREE BELGIQUE

PREPARATION TIME: 20-25 MINUTES
YIELD: 6-8 SERVINGS

1 tablespoon canola oil
1 small onion, minced
2 medium potatoes, diced
4 cups chicken bouillon
3 teaspoons sugar
10 ounces Brussels sprouts
¾-1 cup low-fat milk
salt and pepper to taste
1 cup croutons

Like many purees, this is delicious either hot or cold. To serve cold, cover and chill for at least four hours after adding the milk and the seasonings.

Heat the oil in a large covered saucepan and sauté the onion until soft. Add the potatoes, the bouillon, the sugar, and the Brussels sprouts.

Bring to a boil, lower the heat, cover, and simmer for about 20 minutes, or until tender.

Remove from the heat and cool slightly. Puree in a blender or processor.

Return the puree to the saucepan. Stir in the milk. Season to taste with the salt and pepper.

Reheat to just under a boil, sprinkle with croutons, and serve.

CASHEW, KALE, AND CABBAGE SOUP

PREPARATION TIME: 10-15 MINUTES
COOKING TIME: 1 ½-2 HOURS
YIELD: 4-6 SERVINGS

2 tablespoons canola oil
1 small onion, diced
1 cup shredded cabbage
1 cup chopped kale
1 cup grated carrots
1 medium cooking apple, peeled,
   cored, and diced
6 cups beef broth
⅛ cup tomato paste
¼ cup brown rice
salt and pepper to taste
½ cup cashews
½ cup golden raisins

Cousin Mary Kaye suggested the cashews and natural brown rice in this unusual soup. With vegetables and fruit added, it is hearty enough to serve as a main course.

Heat the oil in a large covered saucepan and sauté the onion, the cabbage, the kale, and the carrots until limp. Add the apple.

Gradually stir in the beef broth and blend in the tomato paste. Add the rice.

Cover and simmer for at least 1 hour.

Check the seasonings and add the salt and pepper to taste. Stir in the cashews and the raisins, and continue cooking until the raisins have plumped.

Remove from the heat and serve.

HEARTY CAULIFLOWER SOUP

PREPARATION TIME: 30-40 MINUTES
YIELD: 4 SERVINGS

As long ago as the sixth century B.C., cooks in ancient Rome were preparing and serving cauliflower—a cultivated cousin of the cabbage—in side dishes and hearty soups like this one.

10 ounces cauliflowerets
$1/8$ cup minced onions
2 cups chicken broth
1 tablespoon canola oil
$1/8$ cup all-purpose flour
1 cup low-fat milk
1 tablespoon minced parsley
salt and pepper to taste
paprika to taste
nutmeg

Place the cauliflower in a large covered saucepan with the onions and the broth. Cover and simmer about 15 minutes, or until tender.

Remove from the heat, cool slightly, and puree in a blender or processor. Return the puree to the saucepan over low heat.

Combine the oil and the flour in a small saucepan and cook over medium heat until bubbly. Add the milk and cook until thick, stirring constantly to prevent lumps. Stir into the puree, blending well.

Stir the parsley through the puree. Check the seasonings, adding the salt, pepper, and paprika to taste. Dust lightly with the nutmeg. Serve.

SCOTS BROTH

PREPARATION TIME: 10-15 MINUTES
COOKING TIME: 2 ½-3 HOURS
YIELD: 6-8 SERVINGS

¾ **pound extra-lean lamb, cubed**
8-10 cups water
¼ **cup raw barley**
1 medium turnip, diced
1 medium potato, diced
2 medium carrots, coined
1 medium onion, minced
1 ½ **cups chopped cabbage**
¼ **cup minced parsley**
salt and pepper to taste

Heat a large covered saucepan over medium-high heat until a drop of water dances on the surface. Sear the lamb on all sides.

Add 8 cups of the water, and the barley. Bring to a boil, lower the heat, and simmer covered for at least 1 ½ hours.

Add the turnip, the potato, the carrots, the onion, and the cabbage and continue to simmer covered for at least 1 hour, adding water if too thick.

Stir in the parsley, check the seasonings, and add the salt and pepper to taste.

Simmer uncovered for 10 minutes, ladle into a tureen or individual bowls, and serve.

JACK'S FAVORITE BROCCOLI PUREE

PREPARATION TIME: 25-30 MINUTES
YIELD: 4 SERVINGS

3 cups chicken bouillon or broth
3 cups broccoli pieces
1 stalk celery, diced
¼ cup minced onions
1-2 cups low-fat milk
salt and pepper to taste
4 thin lemon slices

The broccoli that forms the base for this delicate puree is of the standard sprouting type that originated in Italy and is sometimes called Italian asparagus.

Bring the bouillon or broth to a boil in a large covered saucepan. Add the broccoli, the celery, and the onions.

Cook, covered, until tender. Remove from the heat, cool slightly, and puree in a blender or processor.

Return the puree to the saucepan, stir in the milk to thin it to your liking, and add the salt and pepper to taste. Reheat to just under a boil.

Place a slice of lemon in each soup plate, add the puree, and serve.

SISTER'S SOUP

PREPARATION TIME: 15-20 MINUTES
COOKING TIME: 1 ½-2 HOURS
YIELD: 4-6 SERVINGS

½ **pound extra-lean beef, cubed**
½ **cup minced onions**
6-8 cups beef bouillon
1 small bay leaf
1 cup grated carrots
2 cups cauliflower pieces
2 cups Brussels sprouts
¾ **cup rotini pasta**
1 teaspoon all-purpose flour
2 tablespoons tomato sauce
salt and pepper to taste

When Sister's people came to this country from Yugoslavia, they brought with them their love of Broccoli & Company vegetables. This soup features some of their favorites—vitamin C-rich cauliflower and Brussels sprouts—along with beta-carotene-rich carrots, tender lean beef, and a hearty broth.

Put a medium covered saucepan over medium-high heat and sauté the beef and the onions until the beef is brown and the onions are limp.

Add 6 cups of the bouillon and the bay leaf and bring to a boil. Add the carrots, the cauliflower, the Brussels sprouts, and the pasta. Lower the heat to simmer and cook, covered, for at least 1 hour, stirring occasionally.

Blend the flour and the tomato sauce in a small mixing bowl. Add to the cauliflower mixture, stirring constantly to prevent lumps. Add more bouillon if too thick.

Continue to simmer for at least 20 minutes, stirring occasionally.

Remove the bay leaf and discard. Check the seasonings and add the salt and pepper to taste. Serve.

PUREE OF WINTER GREENS

PREPARATION TIME: 40-45 MINUTES
YIELD: 4-6 SERVINGS

4 cups chicken bouillon
1 ½ cups shredded kale
1 cup shredded mustard greens
1 cup shredded collards
2 cups shredded cabbage
4 scallions, chopped
¼ cup minced parsley
3 tablespoons canola oil
3 tablespoons all-purpose flour
1-2 cups low-fat milk
salt and pepper to taste

Though we call it Winter Greens, the ingredients in this hearty, dark green puree are always available in supermarkets, so it can be prepared and served at any time of the year.

Bring the bouillon to a boil in a large covered saucepan. Add the kale, the mustard greens, the collards, the cabbage, the scallions, and the parsley.

Lower the heat to simmer, cover, and cook until tender, lifting the lid occasionally.

Remove from the heat and cool slightly. Puree in a blender or processor until smooth.

Return the kale mixture to the saucepan and keep warm.

In another saucepan, blend the oil and the flour and cook until bubbly. Add 1 cup of the milk and cook until thick, stirring constantly to prevent lumps.

Fold the milk mixture into the reserved kale mixture, adding more milk if too thick.

Blend well and reheat to just under a boil. Check the seasonings. Add the salt and pepper to taste. Serve.

CHUNKY CAULIFLOWER SOUP

PREPARATION TIME: 45-50 MINUTES
YIELD: 6-8 SERVINGS

This soup, rich with chunky morsels of tender cauliflower, is worth every precious minute you put into its preparation. For maximum convenience, make it ahead of time up to the point where the bay leaf is removed. Continue preparation when ready to add last two ingredients and to reheat before serving.

1 tablespoon canola oil
¼ cup minced onions
1 medium carrot, finely grated
½ cup minced celery
10 ounces cauliflowerets
2 tablespoons minced parsley,
    divided
4 cups chicken broth
¼ teaspoon herbal seasoning
1 small bay leaf
2 tablespoons soft margarine or butter
⅓ cup all-purpose flour
2 ¼ cups low-fat milk
salt and pepper to taste
¼ cup sour cream
¼ cup plain low-fat yogurt

Heat the oil in a large covered saucepan and sauté the onions until limp. Add the carrot and the celery and sauté 5 minutes.

Turn heat to low, add the cauliflower and 1 tablespoon of the parsley. Cover and cook 15 minutes, stirring occasionally.

Add the broth, the herbal seasoning, and the bay leaf to the cauliflower mixture. Cover and continue to cook over low heat.

Melt the margarine or butter in a medium saucepan, stir in the flour, and cook until bubbly. Add the milk, stirring constantly to prevent lumps. Cook until thick and smooth. Add to the cauliflower mixture.

Season to taste with the salt and pepper and simmer for 15-20 minutes, stirring frequently. Remove the bay leaf.

Fold in the sour cream and the yogurt and reheat to just under a boil.

Sprinkle with the remaining 1 tablespoon of parsley, and serve.

MICHIGAN BEAN AND TURNIP SOUP

PREPARATION TIME: 25-35 MINUTES
YIELD: 4-6 SERVINGS

We would be glad to match this recipe against the famous bean soup regularly featured on the luncheon menu, offered to senators in their private dining rooms in Washington, D.C. In addition to hearty Michigan navy beans for flavor, protein, and bulk, our soup is improved by vitamin C-rich turnips.

2 small-medium turnips
2 cups cooked Michigan navy beans
   with cooking liquid, divided
1 tablespoon minced onions
2 tablespoons minced parsley
1 ½-2 cups low-fat milk
salt and pepper to taste

Cook the turnips in a medium covered saucepan in as little water as possible. Drain and discard liquid.

Combine the turnips with 1 cup of the beans and all of the bean liquid in a blender or processor. Add the onion and the parsley. Blend until smooth.

Turn the turnip mixture back into the saucepan, add the remaining 1 cup of beans, 1 ½ cups of the milk, and the salt and pepper to taste.

Cover and simmer over low heat for 15-20 minutes, stirring occasionally.

Add the remaining milk if too thick. Reheat, check the seasonings, and serve.

NEW ENGLAND TURNIP CHOWDER

PREPARATION TIME: 30-45 MINUTES
YIELD: 4-6 SERVINGS

1 cup diced turnips
2 cups diced potatoes
1 small carrot, diced
¼ cup diced onions
¼ cup diced celery
2-4 cups low-fat milk
1 16-ounce can creamed corn
6 ½-ounce can chopped clams with
   liquid
pinch cumin
pinch sage
pinch rosemary
salt and pepper to taste

We usually make this hearty chowder a day or two ahead so it can "ripen" as a good chowder should. (However, unable to resist having some the day it's made, we double the recipe: Half to eat at once; half for later, warmed up.)

In a medium covered saucepan, cook the turnips for 15-20 minutes, or until tender, in as little water as possible. Drain, discard cooking liquid, and set turnips aside.

In a large covered saucepan, combine the potatoes, the carrot, the onions, and the celery. Add water to cover, bring to a boil, and cook covered, for 15-20 minutes, or until tender.

Stir in 2 cups of the milk, the reserved turnips, the corn, the clams with liquid, the cumin, the sage, and the rosemary. Add additional milk if needed for proper consistency.

Cover and simmer very gently for 15-20 minutes, stirring occasionally. Check the seasonings and add the salt and pepper to taste.

Remove from the heat and serve or, if storing to "ripen," let cool to room temperature, turn into a covered glass or plastic container and chill.

An hour or so before you are ready to serve, heat in a saucepan to just under a boil over very low heat, stirring occasionally. Serve.

DANISH DUMPLING SOUP

PREPARATION TIME: 35-40 MINUTES
YIELD: 4-6 SERVINGS

It's difficult to make a good soup unless you have a good base to start from, especially when preparing a delicate broth for dumplings. We recommend either making your own stock or bouillon, or buying the best canned or frozen product you can find.

6 cups beef stock or bouillon
½ pound extra-lean ground beef
1 scallion, finely chopped
⅛ teaspoon freshly ground gingerroot
½ teaspoon canola oil
1 teaspoon cornstarch
2 teaspoons soy sauce
1 egg
⅛ cup plus 1 tablespoon water
¾ cup plus 1 tablespoon all-purpose flour
½ teaspoon salt, or to taste
3 cups very finely minced cabbage

Put the stock or bouillon in a large covered saucepan and bring to a boil.

In a medium mixing bowl, combine the ground beef, the scallion, the gingerroot, the oil, the cornstarch, and the soy sauce. Mix thoroughly, shape into balls the size of large marbles, and drop carefully into the broth.

Cook meatballs for 10 minutes. Remove and set aside.

Beat the egg and the water together in a small mixing bowl, add the flour and the salt and stir together until the dough cleans the sides of the bowl.

Drop by teaspoonsful into the broth. Cook for 10 minutes, or until the dumplings rise to the surface. Remove and set aside.

Stir the cabbage into the broth and cook for 10-15 minutes, or until crisp-tender.

Add the reserved meatballs and the reserved dumplings. Cover and simmer over low heat for 5-10 minutes, or until heated through. Serve.

SWISS CHEESE SOUP

PREPARATION TIME: 45-60 MINUTES
YIELD: 4-6 SERVINGS

Nutmeg and Swiss cheese give a hint of fondue flavor to this sturdy, delicious soup featuring cabbage and brown rice.

1 tablespoon soft margarine
1 small or ½ large cabbage, cored, shredded, and chopped
1 small onion, minced
6 cups beef bouillon
⅛ teaspoon nutmeg
⅓ cup raw brown rice
salt and pepper to taste
Swiss cheese, grated

Melt the margarine in a large covered saucepan. Stir in the cabbage and the onion, cover, and cook over medium-low heat until limp, stirring frequently.

Add the bouillon and the nutmeg. Simmer covered for 15 minutes.

Stir in the rice, return to a boil, cover, and cook over low heat for 25-30 minutes, or until tender.

Check the seasonings. Add the salt and pepper to taste.

Ladle into a tureen or individual plates and sprinkle with the cheese. Serve.

SALADS & DRESSINGS

"It's broccoli, dear."
*"I say it's spinach, and I say
the hell with it."*

—Cartoon caption by E.B. White

COMPANY COLESLAW

PREPARATION TIME: 10-15 MINUTES
CHILLING TIME: 1 HOUR
YIELD: 4-6 SERVINGS

1 Golden Delicious apple, cored and
   diced
1 cup mandarin orange sections
2 cups finely shredded cabbage
1 cup cooked carrot coins
¼ cup lemon-flavored low-fat yogurt
¼ cup *Lemonnaise* (see page 49)
1 tablespoon brown sugar
¼ teaspoon nutmeg
shredded lettuce

Though some people serve salads late in the meal, or along with the entrée and side dishes, we usually make it our first course for a number of reasons: Salad greens, including those in BROCCOLI & COMPANY, are most nutritious when first cut; we tend to eat more salad at the beginning of the meal when our appetites are best, than we would if it were left to the middle or the end; and salads have fewer calories than many other dishes, helping our efforts at weight control.

Combine the apple pieces, the mandarin sections, the cabbage, and the carrots in a large mixing bowl. Set aside.

Blend the yogurt, the *Lemonnaise*, the sugar, and the nutmeg in a small mixing bowl. Pour over the cabbage mixture and toss gently until well mixed. Cover, chill 1 hour, and serve on the shredded lettuce.

LEMONNAISE

PREPARATION TIME: 10-15 MINUTES
YIELD: ABOUT 1 CUP

1 egg white
½ teaspoon dry mustard
½ teaspoon sugar
⅛ teaspoon salt, or to taste
1 cup canola oil
1 ½ tablespoons lemon juice
½ tablespoon hot water

Combine the egg white, the mustard, the sugar, and the salt in a deep mixing bowl and beat together until frothy.

Gradually add half the oil, pouring slowly in a thin stream with the mixer running. Slowly add 1 tablespoon of the lemon juice, mixing constantly.

With the mixer running, dribble in the remaining half of the oil and the remaining ½ tablespoon of the lemon juice. Add the hot water and continue to mix until thoroughly blended and the mixture has the color and consistency of prepared mayonnaise.

The *Lemonnaise* may be used at once, or stored in a covered glass or plastic container in the refrigerator. It will keep just like commercial mayonnaise.

TOSSED BEANS AND GREENS

PREPARATION TIME: 10-15 MINUTES
CHILLING TIME: 2 HOURS
YIELD: 4-6 SERVINGS

1 cup cooked carrot coins
1 cup finely chopped raw young kale
   leaves
1 cup raw broccoli florets
1 cup cooked kidney beans
¼ cup minced green pepper
½ cup diced celery
¼ cup minced green onions
Lemonnaise Green (see page 51)
¼ cup cubed low-fat cheese
¼ cup croutons
¼ cup garbanzo beans, drained
lettuce leaves

The kale featured in this nutritious salad traces its roots back some thousands of years to origins in areas of the eastern Mediterranean or Asia Minor. Kale was known by both Greeks and Romans long before the Christian era, prized for its nutritional and medicinal value.

In a large mixing bowl, combine the carrots, the kale, the broccoli, the kidney beans, the green pepper, the celery, and the onions. Add enough *Lemonnaise Green* to moisten. Toss gently.

Cover and chill for 2 hours. Sprinkle with the cheese cubes, the croutons, and the garbanzo beans. Serve on the crisp lettuce leaves.

LEMONNAISE GREEN

PREPARATION TIME: 5-10 MINUTES
CHILLING TIME: 2 HOURS
YIELD: ABOUT 1 CUP

¼ cup cooked broccoli
¼ cup cooked kale
1 tablespoon fresh parsley
1 tablespoon fresh chives
1 teaspoon fresh tarragon
1 teaspoon fresh chervil
1 teaspoon fresh dill
¾ cup *Lemonnaise* (see page 49)
salt and pepper to taste

We've combined the tang of Lemonnaise *(see page 49) with the mellow flavor and bright color of broccoli and kale for one of the best dressings ever. Serve over tossed salads and slaws or as a dip for crudités.*

Combine the broccoli, the kale, the parsley, the chives, the tarragon, the chervil, and the dill in a blender or processor and blend until smooth.

Add the *Lemonnaise* and the salt and pepper to taste and blend until well mixed.

Turn into a covered glass or plastic container and chill for 2 hours before using.

CELERY SEED DRESSING

PREPARATION TIME: 5-10 MINUTES
YIELD: ABOUT 1 ½ CUPS

1 cup canola oil
6 tablespoons apple cider vinegar
⅓ cup sugar
1 teaspoon dry mustard
1 teaspoon salt, or to taste
1 tablespoon ground celery seed
1 teaspoon paprika

Combine the oil, the vinegar, and the sugar in a blender or processor and blend until cloudy and thick.

Add the mustard, the salt, the celery seed, and the paprika and continue to blend for 30 seconds.

Remove and use at once, or store in the refrigerator in a covered glass or plastic container. Use within two months.

STOP-AND-GO SALAD

PREPARATION TIME: 15-20 MINUTES
YIELD: 4-6 SERVINGS

½ cup *Lemonnaise* (see page 49)
⅛-¼ cup plain low-fat yogurt
½ cup crushed pineapple
½ cup golden raisins
1 red Delicious apple
½ small green cabbage
½ small red cabbage

Cut and slice the green cabbage and the red cabbage for this colorful salad just before making it. Keep it as cold as possible to retain vitamins.

Combine the *Lemonnaise*, ⅛ cup of the yogurt, the pineapple, and the raisins in a large mixing bowl. Set aside.

Quarter and core the apple, but do not peel. Cut into bite-size cubes and add to the reserved yogurt mixture. Set aside.

Cut the cabbage halves into quarters, remove core wedges, and slice as thin as possible. Add to the reserved apple mixture and toss gently until all ingredients are moistened, adding the remaining yogurt if necessary.

Serve at once, or cover and chill for serving later.

MARINATED CAULIFLOWER

PREPARATION TIME: 15-20 MINUTES
YIELD: 4-6 SERVINGS

10 ounces cauliflowerets
¼ teaspoon sugar
⅛ teaspoon salt, or to taste
dash pepper
1 teaspoon grated lemon zest
1 tablespoon lemon juice
1 tablespoon minced onions
⅛ cup olive oil
1 clove garlic
lettuce
¼ cup thinly sliced green pepper
¼ cup pimento-stuffed green olives,
   sliced
2 hard-cooked eggs, quartered
freshly ground black pepper

Cook the cauliflower in a small covered saucepan in as little water as possible until crisp-tender. Drain and set aside.

Combine the sugar, the salt, the pepper, the lemon zest, the lemon juice, the onions, and the olive oil in a blender or processor and blend until smooth.

Pour the oil mixture over the reserved cauliflower and marinate for at least 30 minutes. Drain, reserving both the cauliflower and the marinade. Set aside.

Cut the garlic clove in two and rub the cut halves over the inside surface of a large salad bowl. Discard the garlic.

Line the salad bowl with lettuce leaves, add the reserved cauliflower, the green pepper, the olives, and the eggs.

Pour enough of the reserved marinade over the cauliflower mixture to moisten, grind pepper over to taste, and serve.

SAUERKRAUT AND POTATO SALAD

PREPARATION TIME: 10-15 MINUTES
YIELD: 4-6 SERVINGS

2 cups cooked cubed potatoes
½ cup cooked carrot coins
¼ cup minced green onion tops
½ cup minced celery
½ cup drained rinsed sauerkraut
salt and pepper to taste
Yogurt Dressing (see below)
salad greens

This is our favorite version of a salad that combines tangy sauerkraut with bland potatoes, orange carrots with green onion tops, and all brought together by a mild mannered Yogurt Dressing *(See below).*

In a large mixing bowl, combine the potatoes, the carrots, the onion tops, the celery, and the sauerkraut.

Salt and pepper to taste, toss with enough *Yogurt Dressing* to moisten, and serve on the crisp salad greens.

YOGURT DRESSING

PREPARATION TIME: 10-15 MINUTES
CHILLING TIME: 4 HOURS
YIELD: 1 ½ CUPS

¾ cup plain low-fat yogurt
¼ cup *Lemonnaise* (see page 49)
¼ cup sour cream
2 tablespoons sugar
½ tablespoon dried minced onions
½ tablespoon dried minced parsley
1 teaspoon Salad Supreme seasoning
salt and pepper to taste

Combine the yogurt, the *Lemonnaise*, the sour cream, the sugar, the onions, the parsley, the seasoning, and the salt and pepper in a blender or processor. Blend until smooth.

Turn into a covered glass or plastic container and chill at least 4 hours. Serve.

SET SALAD SLAW

PREPARATION TIME: 10-15 MINUTES
CHILLING TIME: AT LEAST 4 HOURS
YIELD: 1-QUART MOLD

1 envelope unflavored gelatin
½ cup sugar
1 cup water
½ cup lemon juice
½ cup *Lemonnaise* (see page 49)
⅛ teaspoon salt
1 cup finely shredded cabbage
½ cup finely shredded kale
½ cup finely grated carrots
2 tablespoons minced celery
1 teaspoon minced onions
salad greens

What we call gelatin or molded salads used to be referred to as "set" salads with the "setting" agent—the gelatin—added to a mixture of fruit juice and water. That's the kind of gelatin we prefer, used here as background for cabbage and kale, two of our favorite Broccoli & Company vegetables.

Sprinkle the gelatin and the sugar over the water in a small saucepan and heat, stirring constantly, until *completely* dissolved.

Turn into a medium mixing bowl and add the lemon juice, the *Lemonnaise,* and the salt. Chill until partially set.

Beat the partially set mixture until fluffy. Fold in the cabbage, the kale, the carrots, the celery, and the onions.

Turn into a 1-quart mold or individual molds and chill until firm.

Unmold onto the crisp salad greens and serve.

PATCHWORK SALAD

PREPARATION TIME: 10-15 MINUTES
YIELD: 4-6 SERVINGS

1 clove garlic
1 small head lettuce
1 cup raw cauliflowerets
1 cup raw broccoli florets
½ cup raw green peas
½ cup grated carrots
½ cup cooked whole kernel corn
salad dressing
¼ cup mushroom slices
¼ cup pitted black olives
¼ cup pimiento-stuffed green olives
croutons

Cut the garlic clove in two and rub the inside of a large salad bowl with the cut halves. Discard the garlic.

Tear the lettuce into bite-size pieces and combine in the salad bowl with the cauliflower, the broccoli, the peas, the carrots, and the corn. Add the salad dressing to coat lightly and toss to mix well.

Sprinkle the mushroom slices and the olives over the lettuce mixture. Top with the croutons and serve.

SIDE DISHES

*After the vines came rows of vegetables of all
the kinds that flourish in every season . . .
These were the gifts of heaven.*

—Homer

24 KARAT CASSEROLE

PREPARATION TIME: 15-20 MINUTES
BAKING TIME: 30-40 MINUTES
YIELD: 4-6 SERVINGS

1 ½ cups shredded rutabaga
1 cup shredded carrots
¼ cup light corn syrup
¼ cup soft margarine
½ teaspoon cinnamon
salt to taste
1 orange

Tawny rutabaga, bright orange carrots, and tangy citrus cartwheels are bound together in this unusual dish by a sweet sauce based on pale gold corn syrup and soft brown cinnamon.

Preheat the oven to 350° F. Lightly oil a 1-quart covered casserole dish.

Combine the rutabaga and the carrots in the casserole. Set aside.

In a small saucepan, heat the syrup, the margarine, and the cinnamon until the margarine is melted.

Pour the syrup mixture over the rutabaga mixture, and sprinkle with the salt to taste. Cut the whole orange into thin slices and arrange over the top.

Cover the casserole and bake for 30-40 minutes, or until tender. Remove from the oven and serve.

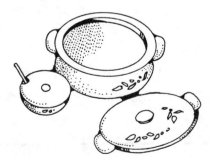

KOHLRABI AU GRATIN

PREPARATION TIME: 20-25 MINUTES
YIELD: 4-6 SERVINGS

1 tablespoon canola oil
1 small onion, minced
2 cups kohlrabi slices
1 cup tomato pieces
salt and pepper to taste
pinch basil
pinch garlic powder
½ cup buttered rye bread crumbs
¼ cup grated low-fat cheese

Heat the oil in a medium covered saucepan. Sauté the onion and the kohlrabi until limp. Cover the pan, lower the heat, and cook until the kohlrabi is crisp-tender. Add the tomatoes and continue cooking until done.

Sprinkle the kohlrabi mixture with the salt and pepper, the basil, and the garlic powder. Stir through the mixture.

Turn into a serving dish, top with the bread crumbs and the cheese, and serve.

CREAMED CABBAGE PARMIGIAN

PREPARATION TIME: 15-20 MINUTES
YIELD: 4-6 SERVINGS

1 small or ½ medium cabbage
1 ½ tablespoons canola oil
2 tablespoons all-purpose flour
1 cup low-fat milk
pinch onion salt
salt and pepper to taste
Parmesan cheese, grated

Leftovers of this dish can be reheated and spooned over baked potato halves with extra Parmesan cheese to taste.

Cut the cabbage into bite-size pieces and cook in a medium saucepan in as little water as possible until crisp-tender. Do not drain. Set aside.

Heat the oil in a medium saucepan and stir in the flour to form a smooth paste. When bubbly, add the milk and cook until smooth and thick, stirring constantly to prevent lumps. Add the onion salt.

Fold the cabbage into the milk mixture, cover, and cook until heated through. Salt and pepper to taste.

Turn into a serving dish, sprinkle with the cheese, and serve.

SWEET GEORGIA CASSEROLE

PREPARATION TIME: 10-15 MINUTES
BAKING TIME: 20-25 MINUTES
YIELD: 4-6 SERVINGS

½ tablespoon canola oil
1 tablespoon all-purpose flour
½ cup low-fat milk
¼ cup grated Parmesan cheese
¼ cup *Lemonnaise* (see page 49)
½ teaspoon lemon juice
1 ½ ounces cream cheese, cubed
1 cup cooked pearl onions
2 cups cooked broccoli pieces

Fresh sweet onions are best in this dish, but if you can't get them, substitute canned, drained pearl onions.

Preheat the oven to 375° F. Oil a 1 ½-quart ovenproof serving dish.
Heat the oil in a small saucepan, stir in the flour, and cook until bubbly. Add the milk gradually, stirring constantly to prevent lumps. When smooth and thick, blend in the Parmesan cheese, the *Lemonnaise*, the lemon juice, and the cream cheese. Remove from the heat and set aside.
Combine the onions and the broccoli in the prepared dish and pour the cheese mixture over them. Bake, uncovered, for 20 minutes, or until bubbly. Remove from the oven and serve.

SAUTÉED TURNIP GREENS

PREPARATION TIME: 15-20 MINUTES
YIELD: 4 SERVINGS

1 tablespoon canola oil
¼ cup minced onions
¼ cup minced green pepper
1 pound turnip greens, chopped
freshly ground black pepper
2 teaspoons lemon juice
½ teaspoon brown sugar

For variety in this recipe, substitute kale, collards, or mustard greens and adjust the cooking time as necessary.

Heat the oil in a large covered frying pan, add the onions and the green pepper, and sauté until tender. Stir in the turnip greens.
Reduce the heat to low, cover, and cook for 10 minutes, or until tender.
Sprinkle with the pepper, the lemon juice, and the sugar.
Toss lightly and serve.

LAYERED KALE CASSEROLE

PREPARATION TIME: 25-30 MINUTES
YIELD: 4-6 SERVINGS

1 ½ cups cooked brown rice
1 cup shredded low-fat cheese
¼ cup minced green onion tops
¼ cup minced celery leaves
1 teaspoon Worcestershire sauce
¼ cup low-fat milk
¼ teaspoon thyme
¼ teaspoon ground sage
¼ teaspoon rosemary
salt and pepper to taste
2 cups cooked chopped kale

It is sometimes difficult to find kale in the produce bins at supermarkets, but produce managers will often special order if asked. The best kale, of course, is that grown in your own garden and picked just before use.

Preheat the oven to 375° F. Oil a 1 ½-quart covered casserole dish.

In a medium mixing bowl, combine the rice, the cheese, the onion tops and the celery leaves with the Worcestershire sauce, the milk, the thyme, the sage, the rosemary, and the salt and pepper to taste. Mix well.

Place half the kale in the prepared casserole dish and spread the rice mixture over evenly. Cover with the remaining kale.

Cover and bake for 15-20 minutes, or until the cheese is melted and bubbling.

Remove from the oven and serve.

CABBAGE WITH RICE

PREPARATION TIME: 20-30 MINUTES
YIELD: 4 SERVINGS

This simple sturdy dish is so delicious that we always double the recipe, knowing we'll each want more than our share when it's ready to eat. We rarely have leftovers, but when we do, we find they're almost better than the original dish.

1 small cabbage
1 ½ cups cooked brown rice
4 tablespoons soft margarine
1 cup grated low-fat cheese
¼ teaspoon grated nutmeg
salt to taste

Shred the cabbage and cook over medium heat until crisp-tender in a large covered saucepan in as little water as possible.

Lower the heat and stir in the rice, the margarine, the cheese, and the nutmeg. Add the salt to taste.

When all ingredients are heated through, turn into a dish and serve.

LEMON BUTTERED BRUSSELS SPROUTS

PREPARATION TIME: 15-20 MINUTES
YIELD: 4 SERVINGS

1 tablespoon soft margarine or butter
½ cup pecan halves
2 cups cooked Brussels sprouts
salt to taste
½ lemon, thinly sliced
freshly ground black pepper

Heat the margarine or butter in a medium covered frying pan. Add the pecans and stir over medium-high heat until lightly toasted.

Add the Brussels sprouts and stir gently to mix with the pecans. Salt to taste.

Reduce the heat to low. Arrange the lemon slices over the Brussels sprouts mixture, cover, and cook for 10 minutes.

Remove the lemon slices, turn the Brussels sprouts mixture into a serving dish, and dust very lightly with pepper. Serve.

CHAMPIT TATTIES AND BASHED NEEPS

PREPARATION TIME: 10-15 MINUTES
BAKING TIME: 25-40 MINUTES
YIELD: 4-6 SERVINGS

1 ½ cups cooked turnips
2 cups cooked sweet potatoes
5 tablespoons plain low-fat yogurt
2 tablespoons grated low-fat cheese
2 tablespoons soft margarine
⅛ teaspoon ground cloves
⅛ teaspoon ground cinnamon
salt to taste

Folks who know what's what in the Highlands would know they were going to get mashed potatoes and mashed turnips if they saw this item on the menu. They might be surprised, however, to find the Tatties orange instead of white.

Preheat the oven to 375° F. Oil a 1-quart casserole dish.

Combine the turnips, the sweet potatoes, the yogurt, the cheese, the margarine, the cloves, and the cinnamon and process or beat until smooth and fluffy, as you would with mashed potatoes. Add the salt to taste.

Turn the turnip mixture into the casserole and bake, covered, for 25 minutes. Uncover and continue baking for 15 minutes, or until crisp on top.

Remove from the oven and serve.

SOUFFLÉ VERT

PREPARATION TIME: 10-15 MINUTES
BAKING TIME: 45-60 MINUTES
YIELD: 4-6 SERVINGS

2 ½ tablespoons canola oil
4 tablespoons all-purpose flour
salt and pepper to taste
1 cup low-fat milk
3 eggs, separated
2 cups cooked chopped greens

We make this Soufflé *with kale, collards, and mustard or turnip greens, depending on what we have on hand. As with all dark green leafy vegetables, these members of* BROCCOLI & COMPANY *are rich in beta-carotene, fiber, and vitamin C.*

Preheat the oven to 350° F. In a shallow baking pan, put 1 inch of hot water and place the pan in the oven. Oil a 1-1 ½-quart soufflé pan.

Combine the oil, the flour, and the salt and pepper in a medium saucepan and stir until smooth and bubbly. Add the milk and cook until thick, stirring constantly to prevent lumps. Remove from the heat and set aside.

Beat the egg whites to stiff peaks in a large mixing bowl. Set aside.

In a blender or processor, puree the egg yolks, the greens, and the reserved milk mixture. Fold into the reserved egg whites until completely blended.

Turn into the prepared soufflé pan and set into the water in the baking pan. Bake for 45-60 minutes, or until a tester inserted in the center comes out clean.

Remove from the oven and serve immediately.

CRACKERI BROCCOLI

PREPARATION TIME: 10-15 MINUTES
BAKING TIME: 20-25 MINUTES
YIELD: 4-6 SERVINGS

20 ounces broccoli spears
2 tablespoons canola oil
2 tablespoons all-purpose flour
low-fat milk
salt and pepper to taste
¼ cup shredded Gruyère cheese
½ cup fine saltine cracker crumbs

Preheat the oven to 375° F. Oil a 1-1 ½-quart casserole dish.

Cook the broccoli in a medium covered saucepan in as little water as possible until tender. Drain, reserve, and set aside the cooking liquid. Arrange the broccoli in the casserole dish. Set aside and keep warm.

Heat the oil in a small saucepan and blend in the flour. Stir in the reserved broccoli liquid and enough milk to make 1 cup. Cook to the consistency of a medium white sauce, stirring constantly to prevent lumps. Add milk if too thick.

Check the seasonings and add the salt and pepper to taste.

Pour the milk mixture over the reserved broccoli and sprinkle with the cheese and the crumbs. Bake for 20-25 minutes, or until golden brown and bubbly.

Remove from the oven and serve.

BAKED RUTABAGA CROQUETTES

PREPARATION TIME: 10-15 MINUTES
BAKING TIME: 25-30 MINUTES
YIELD: 4-6 SERVINGS

¾ cup fine saltine cracker crumbs
dash allspice
¼ cup minced green onions
½ cup grated low-fat cheddar cheese
2 egg whites
1 cup cooked mashed rutabaga
3 cups mashed potatoes
2 tablespoons soft margarine
salt and pepper to taste
parsley sprigs

Preheat oven to 375° F. Oil or line 8 muffin tins.

Mix the crumbs, the allspice, the onions, and the cheese in a small mixing bowl. Set aside.

In a large mixing bowl, beat together the egg whites, the rutabaga, the potatoes, the margarine, and the salt and pepper to taste.

Scoop the rutabaga mixture by half cups, roll in the reserved crumb mixture, and place in the prepared muffin tins.

Bake for 25-30 minutes, or until golden brown and crusty. Remove from the oven, turn out of the tins, and garnish with parsley sprigs. Serve.

BRAISED KALE

PREPARATION TIME: 15-20 MINUTES
YIELD: 4 SERVINGS

1 tablespoon canola oil
¼ cup diced green onions
1 stalk celery, minced
1 pound kale, coarsely chopped
⅛ teaspoon garlic powder, or to taste
chicken or beef broth
salt and pepper to taste

Turnip tops, mustard greens, or collards may be used in place of the kale called for in this recipe.

Heat the oil in a medium covered frying pan and sauté the onions and the celery until crisp-tender.

Add the kale, the garlic powder, and enough broth to prevent burning. Stir and toss to mix thoroughly.

Cover and cook for 10-15 minutes, or until the kale is tender. Do not overcook.

Salt and pepper to taste and serve.

DILLED BROCCOLI

PREPARATION TIME: 15-20 MINUTES
YIELD: 4-6 SERVINGS

4 tablespoons soft margarine
2 green onions, minced
4 tablespoons all-purpose flour
1 teaspoon crushed dill seed, or to
    taste
1 ½-2 cups low-fat milk
salt and pepper to taste
16 ounces broccoli spears
parsley, minced

Melt the margarine in a medium saucepan and sauté the onions until limp. Stir in the flour and the dill seed to make a smooth paste.

Gradually add 1 ½ cups of milk and bring to a boil. Cook until thick, stirring constantly to prevent lumps. Add more milk if too thick, and the salt and pepper to taste.

Turn heat to lowest setting and keep warm.

Cook the broccoli until crisp-tender. Drain and arrange on a serving plate.

Pour the dill seed combination over the broccoli, garnish with a dusting of minced parsley, and serve.

BROCCOLI, PASTA, AND PARMESAN

PREPARATION TIME: 20-25 MINUTES
YIELD: 4-6 SERVINGS

3 tablespoons olive oil
1 clove garlic, crushed
2 cups cooked drained broccoli pieces
2 cups cooked fettucine or other pasta
¾ cup grated Parmesan cheese
salt and pepper to taste

The major ingredients of this recipe all have Italian accents, from the broccoli whose name is Italian for arms or branches, to the pasta for which Italy is famous, to the cheese that originated in the region of Parma, Italy.

Heat the olive oil in a large frying pan and sauté the garlic clove until golden brown. Remove and discard.

Add the broccoli to the pan, shaking and stirring for 5-10 minutes, or until heated through.

Add the pasta and stir until heated through.

Turn onto a platter and sprinkle with the cheese and the salt and pepper to taste. Serve.

CURRIED KOHLRABI

PREPARATION TIME: 25-30 MINUTES
YIELD: 4-6 SERVINGS

1 tablespoon canola oil
2 small onions, thinly sliced
1 ½ pounds kohlrabi, thinly sliced
¼ teaspoon coriander
¼ teaspoon cumin
¼ teaspoon curry powder, or to taste
pinch ground ginger
2 teaspoons sugar
¾ cup plain low-fat yogurt
salt and pepper to taste

For a slightly different taste, substitute turnips or rutabagas for the kohlrabi called for below. Use only fresh, young, tender bulbs for the best results.

Heat the oil in a medium saucepan and sauté the onions and kohlrabi for 10 minutes, or until lightly browned.

Combine the coriander, the cumin, the curry powder, the ginger, the sugar, and the yogurt in a small mixing bowl. Add to the kohlrabi mixture, cover, and cook over low heat for 15-20 minutes, or until the kohlrabi is tender.

Remove from the heat, add the salt and pepper to taste, and serve.

COUNTRY-STYLE GREENS

PREPARATION TIME: 15-20 MINUTES
YIELD: 4 SERVINGS

1-1 ½ pounds young turnip, mustard
　or collard greens, or kale
1 beef bouillon cube
pinch paprika
pinch cayenne pepper
water
salt and pepper

Beef bouillon gives this dish a traditional Southern flavor—without the traditional fatty salt pork.

Tear the greens into bite-size pieces and place in a large covered saucepan with the bouillon cube, the paprika, and the cayenne pepper, adding as little water as possible to prevent burning.

Cover and bring to a boil. Uncover and toss with a fork to ensure that the bouillon cube dissolves completely.

Cover again and simmer for 6-10 minutes, or until tender. Remove from the heat and add the salt and pepper to taste. Turn into a dish and serve.

COMPANY CAULIFLOWER

PREPARATION TIME: 30-45 MINUTES
YIELD: 4-6 SERVINGS

1 medium cauliflower
3 tablespoons canola oil
½ pound mushrooms, sliced
¼ cup diced green onions
¼ cup all-purpose flour
1 ½ cups low-fat milk
salt and pepper to taste
¾ cup grated low-fat cheese

Pay no attention to the name of this recipe and make it often for yourself, or your family: It's too good to reserve just for company!

Preheat the oven to 375° F. Oil a 1-2-quart ovenproof serving dish.

Break the cauliflower into florets and cook in a medium saucepan in a minimum of water. Drain and set aside.

In a small frying pan, heat the oil and sauté the mushrooms and the onions until tender. Remove and set aside.

Blend the flour into the remaining oil and add the milk, stirring constantly until smooth and thick. Salt and pepper to taste.

Put half the reserved cauliflower into the casserole, add half the reserved mushrooms and onions, and half the cheese. Repeat.

Pour the milk mixture over the cauliflower mixture, place the casserole in the oven, and bake for 15-20 minutes, or until golden brown and bubbly. Remove from the oven and serve.

COLIFLOR ESPAÑOL

PREPARATION TIME: 15-20 MINUTES
YIELD: 4-6 SERVINGS

2 cups cauliflowerets
1 tablespoon canola oil
1 small onion, minced
1 small clove garlic
1 cup peeled chopped tomatoes
salt and pepper to taste
¼ cup minced parsley
¼-½ cup grated Colby cheese

This is one of the best and brightest dishes we've ever tasted, combining the tangy red of tomatoes, the delicate white of cauliflower, and the sturdy gold of a medium cheese.

Cook the cauliflower in a medium saucepan in as little water as possible until crisp-tender. Drain and set aside.

Heat the oil in a medium frying pan and sauté the onion until translucent. Press the garlic clove and add the essence to the onion along with the reserved cauliflower.

Cook until the cauliflower is lightly browned, shaking and stirring to prevent burning. Add the tomatoes and the salt and pepper and cook for 5 more minutes.

Turn into a dish, sprinkle with the parsley and the cheese, and serve.

HERBED BAKED GREENS

PREPARATION TIME: 35-40 MINUTES
YIELD: 4-6 SERVINGS

2 egg whites
1 tablespoon canola oil
½ teaspoon Worcestershire sauce
⅓ cup lemon juice
¼ teaspoon crushed rosemary
salt to taste
3 cups cooked chopped collards
2 tablespoons minced onions
2 cups cooked brown rice
1 ½ cups grated low-fat cheese
aluminum foil

Kale, mustard greens, or turnip tops may be substituted for the collards in this recipe.

Preheat the oven to 350° F. Oil an 8-inch square glass baking pan.

In a large mixing bowl, beat the egg whites together with the oil, the Worcestershire sauce, the lemon juice, the rosemary, and the salt. Fold the collards, the onions, the rice, and the cheese into the egg-white mixture.

Turn into the prepared pan, cover tightly with the foil, and bake for 25 minutes. Remove the foil and bake 10-15 minutes, or until slightly brown.

Remove from the oven, cut into squares, and serve.

BRAISED BRUSSELS SPROUTS

PREPARATION TIME: 10-15 MINUTES
COOKING TIME: 20-30 MINUTES
YIELD: 4 SERVINGS

16 ounces Brussels sprouts
beef broth
1 carrot, coined
1 medium onion, diced
1 leek, diced
1 stalk celery, diced
cheesecloth for *bouquet garni*
1 small clove garlic
3 peppercorns
1 whole clove
2 sprigs parsley
1 bay leaf
1 sprig thyme
salt to taste

We save the drained-off broth from this dish to use later as part of the liquid in one of our favorite soups. See pages 31-45 for soup recipes.

Place the Brussels sprouts in a medium covered saucepan with enough broth to cover. Add the carrot, the onion, the leek, and the celery.

Make a *bouquet garni* by tying together in the cheesecloth the garlic, the peppercorns, the clove, the parsley, the bay leaf, and the thyme. Add this bag to the Brussels sprouts mixture.

Bring to a boil, cover, and simmer for 10-20 minutes, or until tender. Check the seasonings and add the salt to taste.

Remove the *bouquet garni*, drain the Brussels sprouts, and reserve the broth for other uses (see above). Serve.

SKILLET-SCALLOPED TURNIPS

PREPARATION TIME: 25-30 MINUTES
YIELD: 4 SERVINGS

1 tablespoon canola oil
4 medium turnips, peeled and diced
1 cup beef broth
1 tablespoon minced parsley
1 green onion, minced
dash garlic powder
1 cup cubed French bread
salt and pepper to taste

For a slightly different taste, use kohlrabi or rutabagas in place of the turnips called for, and proceed as directed.

Heat the oil in a large covered frying pan and sauté the turnips until light golden brown. Add the broth.

Cover the pan and simmer for 15-20 minutes, or until tender and nearly dry.

Sprinkle with the parsley, the onion, and the garlic powder. Add the cubed bread and gently stir until well mixed and heated.

Check the seasonings and add the salt and pepper to taste. Turn into a dish and serve.

OLD-COUNTRY COLCANNON

PREPARATION TIME: 25-30 MINUTES
YIELD: 4-6 SERVINGS

½ tablespoon canola oil
3 green onions, minced
3 cups cooked chopped cabbage
2 ½ cups mashed potatoes
⅓ cup low-fat milk
salt and pepper to taste
soft margarine or butter
parsley, minced

Some of our ancestors brought the recipe for this dish across the Atlantic when they immigrated here from Scotland and Wales. We have adapted it for modern American cooks.

Preheat the oven to 375° F. Have ready a 1 ½-2-quart ovenproof serving dish.

Heat the oil in a small frying pan and sauté the onions until limp. Set aside.

Combine the cabbage, the potatoes, the milk, and the salt and pepper in a large mixing bowl.

Spread the reserved onions over the bottom of the serving dish. Mound the cabbage mixture over the onions. Bake uncovered for 20-30 minutes, or until bubbly and slightly crusty.

Remove from the oven, dot with the margarine or butter, and sprinkle with the parsley. Serve.

VIENNESE RED CABBAGE

PREPARATION TIME: 10-15 MINUTES
COOKING TIME: 1-1 ½ HOURS
YIELD: 4-6 SERVINGS

1 medium red cabbage
1 tablespoon canola oil
¼ cup tarragon vinegar
½ cup dry red table wine
3 tablespoons brown sugar
3 tablespoons water
1 tart apple, peeled and diced
4 tablespoons raspberry jam
¼ teaspoon ground cloves
¼ teaspoon caraway seeds
salt and pepper to taste

Rotkraut, Rodkal, *Belgian Red*, Surkal, *Cabbage Normand*—all are ethnic names for a dish that features red cabbage, red wine, some kind of jam or jelly, vinegar or lemon juice, apples, and various seasonings such as allspice, cloves, caraway seeds, and sugar. We especially like this adaptation of a version we had in Vienna a couple of years ago, with the cabbage simmered in dry red wine and tarragon vinegar, sweetened with sugar and raspberry jam, spiced with cloves and caraway. Köstlich!

Shred the cabbage. In a large saucepan, heat the oil, add the cabbage, and sprinkle with the vinegar, the wine, the sugar, and the water. Cover and cook over low heat for 1 hour, or until tender. Stir occasionally with a wooden or plastic spoon.

Add the apple pieces, the jam, the cloves, the caraway seeds, and the salt and pepper. Simmer for 15-20 minutes.

Remove from the heat and serve.

PUNCHNEP GOLD

PREPARATION TIME: 30-45 MINUTES
YIELD: 4-6 SERVINGS

1 pound rutabagas
4 tablespoons soft margarine, divided
1 ½ cups water
⅔ cup low-fat milk
1 ½ cups instant potato flakes
freshly ground black pepper

Punchnep purists will no doubt be dismayed to see rutabagas, not turnips, in this traditional Welsh dish. But we urge them to try it our way before they read us—or it—out of the club. A word of warning: Rutabagas are made of sterner stuff than potatoes. Don't try to "mash" them with a hand mixer. We tried that once. The rutabagas won. The next time, we blended them in our food processor, and we won. They came out creamy, as smooth as silk. (P.S. Purists who insist on turnips instead of rutabagas will have to change the title to Punchnep White.*)*

Cook the rutabagas in as little water as possible in a medium covered saucepan for 20-30 minutes, or until tender. Turn into a blender or processor with 2 tablespoons of the margarine and blend until smooth. Set aside and keep warm.

Bring the 1 ½ cups of water, salted to taste, to a boil in a medium covered saucepan. Stir in the remaining 2 tablespoons of margarine, remove from the heat, and add the milk. Stir the potato flakes through the milk mixture with a fork until softened. Do not whip.

Turn the potato mixture into a serving bowl and swirl the reserved rutabaga mixture through for a marbled effect. Dust lightly with pepper and serve.

PAN-SCALLOPED BRUSSELS SPROUTS

PREPARATION TIME: 20-25 MINUTES
YIELD: 4-6 SERVINGS

This dish can be put together in minutes, but it has a lot more going for it than "traditional" fast foods: vitamin C and fiber in both the Brussels sprouts and the potatoes; protein, calcium, and carbohydrates in the cheese sauce.

1 tablespoon canola oil
1 tablespoon soft margarine or butter
2 tablespoons all-purpose flour
2 cups low-fat milk
1 cup shredded low-fat cheese
2 cups cooked Brussels sprouts
1 cup cooked cubed potatoes

Heat the oil and the margarine or butter in a large covered saucepan. Add the flour and cook over medium heat until the mixture bubbles. Gradually stir in the milk and cook until thick, stirring constantly to prevent lumps. Add the cheese and continue stirring until melted.

Add the Brussels sprouts and the potatoes to the cheese mixture. Lower the heat to simmer, cover, and cook until the vegetables are heated through.

Remove from the heat, turn into a dish, and serve.

SALINAS-STYLE KALE

PREPARATION TIME: 10-15 MINUTES
CHILLING TIME: 2 HOURS
YIELD: 4-6 SERVINGS

1 3-ounce package cream cheese,
  softened
½ cup plain low-fat yogurt
3 tablespoons low-fat milk
pinch garlic powder, or to taste
¼ cup pitted ripe olives, sliced
¼ cup pimiento-stuffed green olives,
  sliced
3 cups cooked coarsely chopped kale
2-3 tomatoes, cut into wedges
salad greens
sesame seeds

Many of the Broccoli & Company vegetables grown in this country come from the rich farmlands around Salinas, California, where cooks have developed some unique recipes featuring kale. Particularly good for warm weather meals, this dish can be prepared with collards, mustard greens, or turnip tops as substitutes for the kale.

In a medium mixing bowl, blend the cream cheese with the yogurt, the milk, and the garlic powder until fluffy. Fold in the olives. Cover and chill for at least 2 hours.

Arrange the kale and the tomato wedges in an attractive pattern on the crisp salad greens.

Spoon on the cream cheese mixture, dust with the sesame seeds, and serve.

BRUNCHES & LUNCHES

And he could roast and seethe and boil
and fry, and make a good thick soup,
and bake a pie.

—Chaucer

SCRAMBLE CON CARNE

PREPARATION TIME: 20-25 MINUTES
YIELD: 4-6 SERVINGS

½ **pound extra-lean ground beef**
¼ **cup minced green onions**
1 **cup tomato pieces**
½ **cup cooked carrot coins**
1 **cup cooked kidney beans**
½ **teaspoon chili powder, or to taste**
½ **tablespoon canola oil**
6-8 **eggs**
4-6 **tablespoons tomato juice**
salt and pepper to taste
1 **cup cooked broccoli pieces**
½ **cup grated Monterey Jack cheese**

Sear the beef until brown in a medium covered saucepan. Lower the heat, add the onions, the tomatoes, the carrots, the kidney beans, and the chili powder. Simmer for 15 minutes, stirring occasionally. Set aside and keep warm.

Heat the oil in a large frying pan over medium heat.

In a large mixing bowl, beat the eggs with the tomato juice and the salt and pepper. Turn into the frying pan. Cook, stirring occasionally, until the eggs are firm. Add the broccoli.

Remove from the heat, turn onto a platter, and sprinkle with the cheese.

Serve with the reserved meat mixture in a dish on the side.

MOLDED CORNED BEEF AND CABBAGE SALAD

PREPARATION TIME: 20-30 MINUTES
CHILLING TIME: 4 HOURS
YIELD: 4-6 SERVINGS

1 envelope unflavored gelatin
1 ½ cups water
1 beef bouillon cube
1 tablespoon sugar
2 tablespoons lemon juice
2 tablespoons *Lemonnaise* (see
  page 49)
2 tablespoons sour cream
¾ cup finely shredded cabbage
½ cup cooked diced potatoes
⅛ cup minced green onion tops
¾ cup flaked corned beef
¼ teaspoon prepared mustard
salad greens

Have ready a 1-quart gelatin mold or 4-6 individual molds.

Sprinkle the gelatin over the water in a medium saucepan, add the bouillon cube and the sugar, and stir over low heat until the gelatin, the bouillon cube, and the sugar are *completely* dissolved.

Remove from the heat and let cool to room temperature. Stir in the lemon juice.

Measure 1 cup of the gelatin mixture and set aside. Combine the remaining gelatin in a medium mixing bowl with the *Lemonnaise* and sour cream, beating until blended. Chill.

When the *Lemonnaise* mixture has the consistency of unbeaten egg whites, fold in the cabbage, the potatoes, and the onion tops.

Turn the cabbage mixture into the mold or individual molds. Chill until almost firm.

Chill the reserved 1 cup of gelatin until partially set, then fold in the corned beef and the mustard. Spread the corned beef mixture over the cabbage mixture and chill for 4 hours.

Unmold onto the crisp salad greens and serve.

BROCCOLI AND CHICKEN-FILLED CRÊPES

PREPARATION TIME: 25-35 MINUTES
CHILLING TIME: AT LEAST 1 HOUR
BAKING TIME: 20-30 MINUTES
YIELD: 8-10 CRÊPES

1 egg
¾ cup low-fat milk
1 tablespoon canola oil
½ cup plus 2 tablespoons all-purpose
    flour
¼ teaspoon salt, or to taste
2 tablespoons soft margarine
1 cup chicken broth
1 teaspoon Worcestershire sauce
1 cup grated cheddar cheese
½ cup sour cream
½ cup plain low-fat yogurt
10 ounces broccoli pieces, cooked and
    drained
1 cup cooked chopped chicken

When pressed for time, we make the crêpes for this dish ahead, layer between wax paper sheets in a covered glass or plastic container and chill. As we start the rest of the recipe, we remove the wax paper, stack the crêpes on a plate, and put into a warm oven.

Combine the egg, the milk, the oil, ½ cup of the flour, and the salt in a blender or processor and blend to a smooth batter. Turn into a covered container and chill for at least 1 hour.

Place a crêpe pan or medium frying pan over medium-high heat until a drop of water dances on the surface.

For each crêpe, spoon 2-3 tablespoons of the reserved batter onto the pan, tilting to cover the surface completely. Brown lightly. Stack on a plate and keep warm.

Preheat the oven to 350° F. Have ready an 8 by 8-inch glass baking dish.

In a medium saucepan, combine the margarine and the remaining flour and cook until bubbly. Add the broth and the Worcestershire sauce and cook until thick, stirring constantly. Stir in the cheese until melted.

Remove from the heat and blend in the sour cream and the yogurt. Set aside.

Spoon the broccoli and the chicken equally onto the reserved crêpes and add 1 tablespoon of the reserved sour cream mixture to each. Fold like envelopes and place in the prepared baking dish.

Pour the remaining sour cream mixture over the filled crêpes. Cover with aluminum foil and bake for 20-30 minutes, or until bubbly.

Remove from the oven, remove the foil cover, and serve.

PERFECT PASTA SALAD

PREPARATION TIME: 10-15 MINUTES
CHILLING TIME: AT LEAST 4 HOURS
YIELD: 8-10 SERVINGS

3 tablespoons *Celery Seed Dressing*
  (see page 52)
1 teaspoon prepared mustard
1 tablespoon sugar
5 cups cooked rotini pasta
1 cup cooked broccoli pieces
1 cup cooked carrot coins
½ cup minced onions
1 cup diced celery
1 cup finely shredded cabbage
Lemonnaise **(see page 49)**
plain low-fat yogurt
salt and pepper to taste
4 hard-cooked eggs
salad greens

This rivals our Perfect Potato Salad, *(see page 40 in* SURPRISING CITRUS, A COOKBOOK, *Garden Way Publishing, 1988) for good taste and good nutrition. Simple and straightforward, it keeps well and can be made a day or two before you plan to serve.*

Whisk together the *Celery Seed Dressing*, the mustard, and the sugar in a small mixing bowl. Set aside.

Combine the pasta, the broccoli, the carrots, the onions, the celery, and the cabbage in a large mixing bowl. Pour over and mix through the reserved *Dressing* mixture. Set aside.

Blend enough *Lemonnaise* and yogurt in equal amounts in a small mixing bowl to moisten the pasta mixture. Salt and pepper to taste. Set aside.

Shell the eggs, cut into thin slices, and fold gently through the reserved pasta mixture. Cover and chill for at least 4 hours.

Turn onto the crisp salad greens and serve.

OVEN OMELETTE

PREPARATION TIME: 15-20 MINUTES
BAKING TIME: 30-35 MINUTES
YIELD: 4-6 SERVINGS

4 eggs
1 cup low-fat milk
¼ cup all-purpose flour
1 tablespoon wheat germ
1 ½ cups grated carrots
1 cup grated kohlrabi
2 tablespoons minced green onions
3 tablespoons minced parsley
1 cup grated low-fat cheese
salt and pepper to taste

Resist the temptation to add more milk as you mix this omelette. Both the carrots and the kohlrabi contain a lot of water: It will be released as they cook.

Preheat the oven to 375° F. Oil an 8 by 8 by 2-inch baking pan.

In a large mixing bowl, beat the eggs, the milk, the flour, and the wheat germ until smooth. Stir in the carrots, the kohlrabi, the onions, the parsley, the cheese, and the salt and pepper to taste, mixing well.

Let stand 10 minutes. Stir thoroughly and pour into the prepared baking dish. Bake for 30-35 minutes, or until a knife inserted in the center comes out clean.

Remove from the oven and let stand 5 minutes. Serve.

QUICHE *SANS SOUCI*

PREPARATION TIME: 10-15 MINUTES
BAKING TIME: 30-45 MINUTES
YIELD: 4-6 SERVINGS

2 cups low-fat milk
½ tablespoon canola oil
1 small onion, minced
1 cup cooked diced broccoli
1 cup cooked diced carrots
½ cup cooked cauliflowerets
¾ cup diced low-fat cheese
3 eggs
salt and pepper to taste

Many times we've passed up quiche because we didn't want the fat and the calories in the crust. We decided to see what it would be like without a crust and . . . voila! Nowadays, we make quiche whenever we take a notion, sans crust, sans fat, sans souci.

Preheat the oven to 400° F. Oil a 9-inch pie plate. Scald the milk and set aside to cool slightly.

Heat the oil in a small frying pan and sauté the onions until limp. Place in the prepared pie plate with the broccoli, the carrots, the cauliflowerets, and the cheese.

In a medium mixing bowl, beat together the eggs, the reserved milk, and the salt and pepper. Pour over the broccoli mixture.

Bake for 30-45 minutes, or until a knife inserted in the center comes out clean.

Remove from the oven and let stand for 10 minutes. Serve.

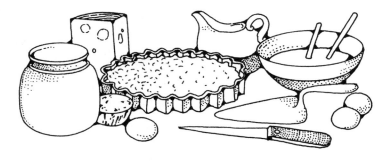

RUSSIAN REUBENS

PREPARATION TIME: 15-20 MINUTES
YIELD: 4 SERVINGS

1 ½ cups drained sauerkraut
⅛ cup minced onions
2 tablespoons minced parsley
⅓ cup *Lemonnaise* (see page 49)
2 tablespoons chili sauce
1 ½ teaspoons prepared mustard
8 large slices Russian black bread
½ pound corned beef, sliced paper-thin
½ pound low-fat Swiss cheese, sliced paper-thin
soft margarine

These unorthodox grilled sandwiches taste their best when teamed with Perfect Pasta Salad and a crisp coleslaw (see pages 83, 48, and 52). Nasdrovia!

In a medium mixing bowl, stir together the sauerkraut, the onions, and the parsley. Set aside.

Blend the *Lemonnaise*, the chili sauce, and the mustard in a small mixing bowl. Spread on the bread. Set aside.

Divide the sauerkraut mixture, the corned beef, and the cheese into four equal portions. Place equally on four of the reserved bread slices. Top with the other four reserved slices of bread.

Set a large frying pan or griddle over medium-high heat.

Spread soft margarine on the tops and bottoms of the sandwiches. Grill on both sides until the bread is crisp and the cheese is melted. Serve.

TEX-MEX OMELETTE

PREPARATION TIME: 20-25 MINUTES
YIELD: 4 SERVINGS

**2 cups canned tomato pieces with
  liquid, divided**
¾ cup broccoli pieces
⅓ cup minced green onions
⅓ cup minced green bell pepper
⅓ cup minced celery
¾ cup cooked pinto beans
salsa to taste
6 eggs
salt and pepper to taste
**¾ cup grated low-fat mozzarella
  cheese**
parsley sprigs

Measure out 6 tablespoons of the tomato liquid and set aside.

Combine the tomatoes, the broccoli, the onions, the green pepper, and the celery in a large covered frying pan. Cook, covered, over medium heat, stirring occasionally, until the celery is tender.

Add the beans and salsa to taste. Reduce the heat to simmer.

In a medium mixing bowl, beat the eggs slightly, then beat in the reserved 6 tablespoons of tomato liquid, and the salt and pepper.

Stir the egg mixture into the broccoli mixture, cover, and cook over medium heat until firm. Sprinkle with the cheese.

Run a spatula around the edges of the pan to loosen the *Omelette*. Slide onto a platter and serve, garnished with the parsley sprigs.

BROCCOLI COMPANY PIE

PREPARATION TIME: 15-20 MINUTES
BAKING TIME: 20-25 MINUTES
YIELD: 4-6 SERVINGS

2 tablespoons canola oil
4 green onions, minced
½ cup chopped kale
1 cup plus 3 tablespoons all-purpose
   flour
1-1 ½ cups chicken broth
⅔ cup plus 2 tablespoons low-fat
   milk
1 cup cooked broccoli pieces
1 cup cooked cauliflowerets
1 cup cooked carrot coins
½ pound fresh mushrooms
salt to taste, divided
pepper to taste
1 ½ teaspoons baking powder
½ teaspoon ground sage
2 tablespoons stick margarine

Good enough for company, this dish is also easy enough for everyday meals. We make it often, especially when we have leftover cooked broccoli, carrots, and cauliflower on hand.

Preheat the oven to 375° F. Have ready a 3-quart soufflé or casserole dish.

Heat the oil in a large saucepan and sauté the onions and the kale until limp. Remove and set aside.

Stir 3 tablespoons of the flour into the oil remaining in the saucepan and cook until smooth and bubbly. Add 1 cup of the broth and ½ cup of the milk. Stir constantly until the mixture has the consistency of a medium white sauce, adding more broth if necessary.

Stir in the reserved onions and kale, the broccoli, the cauliflowerets, the carrots, and the mushrooms. Salt and pepper to taste. Set over low heat to keep warm.

In a medium mixing bowl, stir together the remaining 1 cup of flour, the salt to taste, the baking powder, and the sage. Cut in the margarine until the mixture is like coarse crumbs. Add the remaining milk and stir with a fork until the dough sticks together.

Turn out on a lightly floured surface and knead gently for 30 seconds. Pat into a circle large enough to cover the casserole.

Turn the reserved broccoli mixture into the prepared baking dish. Fit the dough over the top, crimp the edges, and cut several slits so steam can escape.

Bake for 20-25 minutes, or until the crust is golden brown and the filling is bubbling.

Remove from the oven and let stand 10 minutes. Serve.

RHONDA'S CHICKEN AND VEGETABLE CASSEROLE

PREPARATION TIME: 10-15 MINUTES
BAKING TIME: 70-90 MINUTES
YIELD: 4-6 SERVINGS

2 boned chicken breasts, skin and fat
   removed, cut into bite-size pieces
1 cup broccoli pieces
1 cup thin carrot coins
1 cup diced zucchini
1 can cream of mushroom soup
¼ cup low-fat milk
¼ teaspoon paprika, or to taste
salt and pepper to taste
1-1 ½ cups prepared French fried
   onions
aluminum foil

Preheat the oven to 375° F. Lightly oil a 13 by 9 by 2-inch glass baking pan.

Arrange the chicken pieces in the pan and bake, uncovered, for 40-45 minutes, or until done.

Cook the broccoli pieces, the carrot coins, and the zucchini separately in as little water as possible. Drain and set aside.

In a medium mixing bowl, blend together the mushroom soup, the milk, the paprika, and the salt and pepper to taste. Set aside.

Remove the baking pan from the oven and add the vegetables. Pour the reserved soup mixture over the chicken and vegetables and stir together. Sprinkle the French fried onions thickly over the top, cover the baking dish with the aluminum foil, and bake for another 30-35 minutes.

Remove from the oven and serve.

SALAD CHINOISE GENÈVE

PREPARATION TIME: 15-20 MINUTES
YIELD: 8-10 SERVINGS

1 small cabbage, shredded
3 green onions, minced
4 cups cooked cubed chicken
1 cup toasted slivered almonds
¾ cup roasted sunflower seeds
1 cup crumbled dry ramen noodles
¼ cup canola oil
3 tablespoons sweet rice wine
2 tablespoons sugar
1 teaspoon chicken bouillon powder
salt and pepper to taste
salad greens
crackers, toast points, hard rolls

Elegant and hearty, this salad can be accompanied by crackers, toast points, or crusty hard rolls to provide a complete meal.

In a large salad bowl, combine the cabbage and the onions with the chicken, the almonds, the sunflower seeds, and the noodles. Set aside.

In a blender or processor, combine the oil, the wine, the sugar, the bouillon powder, and the salt and pepper. Blend until cloudy and thick. Pour over the reserved chicken mixture and toss.

Spoon onto the crisp salad greens and serve, with the crackers, toast points, or hard rolls on the side.

BROCCOLI RAMEQUINS

PREPARATION TIME: 15-20 MINUTES
BAKING TIME: 30-40 MINUTES
YIELD: 4 SERVINGS

4-8 large mustard leaves
1 cup chicken broth
½ cup whole milk, warmed
4 eggs
1 teaspoon Worcestershire sauce
1 teaspoon lemon juice
½ teaspoon paprika
salt and pepper to taste
2 cups cooked broccoli pieces
1 tablespoon chopped chives
Parmesan cheese, grated

Bright green mustard leaves steamed until pliable are shaped into tangy, attractive, and edible liners for these individual ramequins. Or line an 8-inch ring mold with the wilted greens, increasing baking time if necessary.

Preheat the oven to 325° F. Put a large shallow baking pan with 1 inch of water into the oven to heat. Oil four 4-8-ounce ramequins or an 8-inch ring mold.

Remove stems and thick spines from the greens. Steam until wilted. Mold to fit the insides of the ramequins or the ring mold. Set aside.

In a large mixing bowl, whisk together the broth, the milk, the eggs, the Worcestershire sauce, the lemon juice, the paprika, and the salt and pepper. Fold in the broccoli and the chives.

Turn equally into the prepared ramequins or mold, filling no more than three-quarters full. Sprinkle lightly with the Parmesan cheese and place in the water in the baking pan. Add more hot water if necessary, until level with the filling in the ramequins or mold.

Bake for 30-40 minutes, or until a knife inserted in the center comes out clean.

Remove from the oven and let stand 5 minutes. Serve.

DINNERS & SUPPERS

That night, Best Beloved, they ate wild sheep roasted on the hot stones, and fla-voured with wild garlic and wild pepper; and wild duck stuffed with wild rice and wild fenugreek and wild coriander . . . wild cherries and wild grenadillas. Then the man went to sleep in front of the fire ever so happy; but the woman sat up, comb-ing her hair.

—Rudyard Kipling

TOLTOTT KAPOSZTA

PREPARATION TIME: 25-30 MINUTES
COOKING TIME: 2 ½-4 HOURS
YIELD: 6-8 SERVINGS

The recipe that follows originated in Hungary, where the cabbage is a staple of the national cuisine, as in many northern or temperate zone countries. We often prepare Toltott Kaposzta *for the main dish of a buffet, cooking it in a pan attractive enough to double as a serving dish. It can be made ahead of time, cooled, and stored covered in the refrigerator, then reheated slowly on the stove top or in the oven. We serve it with fluffy brown rice, rye bread, and pumpernickel bread.*

1 large cabbage
boiling water
1 tablespoon canola oil
1 onion, minced and divided
¾ tablespoon paprika
1 small clove garlic, crushed and
   divided
½-1 cup water, divided
2 cups drained sauerkraut; reserve
   liquid
1 tablespoon caraway seeds
1 egg
⅛ cup dry bread crumbs
3 tablespoons uncooked brown rice
1 teaspoon Worcestershire sauce
½ pound extra-lean ground beef
½ pound extra-lean ground pork
salt and pepper to taste

Blanch the cabbage in boiling water to cover for 5 minutes. Drain and cool. Reserve the hot blanching water.

Cut 16-20 of the largest leaves free of the cabbage base and remove carefully to prevent tearing. Reblanch if inner leaves are not supple enough to remove without damage. Drain and cool.

Set the separated leaves and the remaining cabbage aside.

Heat the oil in a large heavy saucepan with a tight-fitting lid and sauté the onion until limp. Remove and set aside 2 tablespoonsful of onions.

Stir the paprika into the remaining onion. Reduce the heat to low. Add half the garlic, ¼ cup of the water, the sauerkraut, and the caraway seeds to the onion mixture. Cover the saucepan and turn the heat to its lowest setting.

Beat the egg in a large mixing bowl, add the reserved onion, the other half of the garlic, the bread crumbs, the rice, the Worcestershire sauce, and ¼ cup of the reserved sauerkraut liquid.

Combine the ground beef, the ground pork, and the salt and pepper to taste. Mix thoroughly into the bread crumb mixture. Set aside.

wooden toothpicks
1 ½ cups sour cream, divided
¾-1 ½ cups beef broth, divided
1 tablespoon all-purpose flour

Cut the thick heavy triangle from the bases of the reserved cabbage leaves and discard the triangles. Place about 2 tablespoons of the meat mixture on each leaf. Fold the sides toward the center over the meat filling and roll or fold into an envelope. Fasten with a toothpick and place on the sauerkraut mixture.

Cut the remainder of the reserved cabbage into quarters. Remove and discard the core. Chop the cabbage coarsely and spread over the filled leaves to cover.

Cover the saucepan and simmer for at *least* 2 hours, adding more water or beef broth as necessary to prevent dryness.

Blend ¾ cup of the sour cream with ¾ cup of the beef broth and the flour, beating until smooth. Pour over the cabbage mixture. Cover and let simmer for another 30 minutes.

Check the seasonings and correct to taste. Remove from the heat and turn into a serving dish, removing and discarding the toothpicks from the filled leaves.

Serve with the remainder of the sour cream on the side.

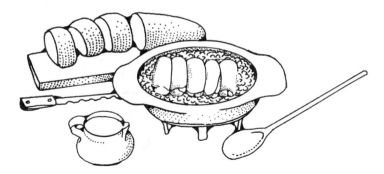

CRASH HASH

PREPARATION TIME: 20-25 MINUTES
YIELD: 4-6 SERVINGS

½ tablespoon canola oil
1 small onion, minced
1 cup cooked diced meat
2 cups cooked cabbage or kale
1 cup cooked carrot coins
3 cups mashed potatoes
salt and pepper to taste

Eating was the last thing on our minds October 19, 1987, as we followed the downward plunge of the Dow Jones Industrial Average. When we did get around to thinking of food, we found a good supply of leftovers in the refrigerator. Crash Hash was the result—a dish so tasty we now make it for dinner even when the stock market goes up!

Heat the oil in a large frying pan and sauté the onion until limp. Add the meat, the cabbage or kale, and the carrots. Spread the potatoes over the meat mixture, pressing firmly. Salt and pepper to taste.

Cook over medium heat until crispy and toasty brown on the underside.

Remove the frying pan from the heat and run a spatula around the inside to loosen the meat mixture. Place a serving platter over the frying pan and invert so the *Hash* comes out bottom side up.

Cut into wedges and serve.

KIM'S STIR-FRIED BROCCOLI AND BEEF

PREPARATION TIME: 15-20 MINUTES
YIELD: 4 SERVINGS

rice
½ **pound flank steak**
2 **teaspoons dry sherry**
2 **teaspoons soy sauce**
salt and pepper to taste
½ **teaspoon brown sugar**
¾ **cup water, divided**
2 **teaspoons cornstarch**
1 **tablespoon canola oil, divided**
1 ½ **pounds broccoli pieces**

This dish can be prepared and ready for guests in mere minutes from start to finish. It features beta-carotene- and vitamin C-rich broccoli and lean beef flank steak. We serve it with side dishes of fluffy rice.

Cook the rice according to package directions. Set aside and keep warm.

Have ready a large frying pan or wok. Slice the flank steak across the grain into narrow 1 ½-inch-long strips and set aside.

Mix the sherry, the soy sauce, the salt and pepper, and the sugar with ½ cup of the water in a small mixing bowl. Set aside.

Blend the cornstarch with the remaining ¼ cup of water in a small mixing bowl. Set aside.

Heat ½ tablespoon of the oil in the frying pan or wok to 300° F. Set the oven to 250° F. and put a serving platter in the oven to warm.

Put the broccoli pieces in the pan or wok, cover, and cook for 2-5 minutes, or until crisp-tender. Turn the broccoli pieces onto the platter and return to the oven to keep warm.

Put the remaining oil in the pan or wok and heat to 375° F. Add the steak strips and stir-fry for 2-5 minutes, or until seared and browned on all sides.

Pour the soy sauce mixture over the steak strips and cook for 2 more minutes.

Return the reserved broccoli to the pan or wok. Add the cornstarch mixture gradually, stirring constantly until thick and clear.

Remove the warmed platter from the oven, turn the broccoli mixture onto it, and serve, with bowls of fluffy rice on the side.

GRANDMA RACHEL'S ROLLED CABBAGE

PREPARATION TIME: 15-20 MINUTES
COOKING TIME: AT LEAST 3 HOURS
YIELD: 4-6 SERVINGS

1 large cabbage
water
1 pound extra-lean ground beef
1 cup cooked brown rice
1 small onion, minced
4 tablespoons brown sugar, divided
1 egg
pinch garlic powder
salt and pepper to taste
wooden toothpicks
1 ½ cups cooked tomatoes
2 cups *Brown Sauce*, divided
   (see page 99)
¾ cup raisins
¼ cup dry bread crumbs
1 teaspoon freshly ground gingerroot
4 tablespoons lemon juice

Made from an old family recipe of some old family friends, this dish is enhanced by freshly ground gingerroot, raisins, and lemon juice to give the vegetables and meat a zesty tang.

Blanch the cabbage in boiling water to cover for 5 minutes. Drain and cool. Reserve the hot blanching water.

Cut 16-20 of the largest leaves free of the cabbage base and remove carefully to prevent tearing. Reblanch if inner leaves are not supple enough to remove without damage. Drain and cool.

Set aside the separated leaves and the remaining cabbage.

Combine the ground beef, the rice, the onion, ½ tablespoon of the brown sugar, the egg, the garlic powder, and the salt and pepper in a large mixing bowl and mix thoroughly.

Cut the thick heavy triangle from the bases of the reserved cabbage leaves and discard the triangles. Place about 2 tablespoons of the meat mixture on each leaf. Fold the sides toward the center over the meat filling and roll or fold into an envelope. Fasten with a toothpick.

Shred the reserved cabbage and place half of it in a large covered saucepan. Lay the reserved stuffed leaves on top and cover with the rest of the shredded cabbage.

Combine the tomatoes, ¾ cup of the *Brown Sauce*, the raisins, the bread crumbs, the gingerroot, the lemon juice, and the remaining 3 ½ tablespoons of brown sugar in a large mixing bowl. Pour over the cabbage mixture. Cover and simmer for at least 3 hours.

Remove the cabbage mixture from the heat, remove the toothpicks from the stuffed leaves, and serve with the remaining *Brown Sauce* on the side.

BROWN SAUCE

PREPARATION TIME: 40 MINUTES
YIELD: ABOUT 2 CUPS

2 cups beef broth
2 tablespoons cornstarch
¼ cup water
salt and pepper to taste

Bring the broth to a boil in a medium saucepan. Stir the cornstarch into the water in a small mixing bowl and add gradually to the broth, stirring constantly to prevent lumps. Continue to stir and cook over medium heat for 2-5 minutes, or until clear and thick. Salt and pepper to taste. Remove from the heat and set aside.

Combine ¾ cup of the *Brown Sauce* with the tomato mixture, (from recipe for Grandma Rachel's Rolled Cabbage). Set the remaining sauce aside until 10-15 minutes before the cabbage mixture is ready to serve. Reheat the reserved sauce, turn into a sauce boat or gravy pitcher, and serve.

HÜHNCHEN MIT BLUMENKOHL

PREPARATION TIME: 20-25 MINUTES
YIELD: 4-6 SERVINGS

1 ½ tablespoons canola oil
3 tablespoons all-purpose flour
2-2 ½ cups chicken broth
pinch celery seed
pinch ground sage
2 tablespoons minced chives
3 cups cooked cubed chicken
3 cups cooked cauliflowerets
salt and pepper to taste
parsley, minced

Heat the oil in a large saucepan, stir in the flour, and cook until bubbly. Add 2 cups of the broth gradually, stirring constantly to prevent lumps. Cook until smooth and thick, adding more broth if necessary. Add the celery seed, the sage, and the chives.

Fold the chicken and the cauliflowerets through the broth mixture. Check the seasonings and add the salt and pepper to taste.

Remove from the heat when piping hot. Turn into a serving dish, dust with the parsley, and serve.

MINNESOTA LAMB STEW

PREPARATION TIME: 15 MINUTES
COOKING TIME: 2-4 HOURS
YIELD: 4-6 SERVINGS

2 tablespoons canola oil
¼ cup all-purpose flour
salt and pepper to taste
¼ teaspoon ground sage
¼ teaspoon ground rosemary
1 ½ pounds lean lamb, cubed
1 bay leaf
4-6 cups water
1 stalk celery, diced
2 medium turnips, cubed
4 medium carrots, diced
3 medium potatoes, cubed
1 medium onion, minced

This is stew the way our relatives and friends in Minnesota like it, with tender lamb and flavorful vegetables in a rich brown sauce that gets better and better the longer it cooks.

Heat the oil in a large, heavy covered saucepan over medium-high heat. Combine the flour, the salt and pepper, the sage, and the rosemary in a plastic or paper bag and shake to mix well. Add the lamb cubes and coat thoroughly.

In the heated saucepan, sear the meat on all sides. Reduce the heat, add the bay leaf and 4 cups of the water, stirring to prevent lumps. Add the celery, the turnips, the carrots, the potatoes, and the onion.

Simmer the lamb mixture covered for 2-4 hours, adding additional water if necessary.

Check the seasonings and remove the stew from the stove. Remove the bay leaf and serve.

ADRIENNE'S CHICKEN HUNGARIAN

PREPARATION TIME: 25-30 MINUTES
YIELD: 4 SERVINGS

Cabbage is a very important source of vitamin C and beta-carotene in countries where less hardy sources of those vital nutrients—such as citrus fruits—are difficult if not impossible to grow under natural conditions. Here, cabbage accompanies delicately flavored braised chicken breasts.

2 chicken breasts, halved
2 tablespoons soft margarine
¼ cup minced onions
1 teaspoon paprika, divided
½ teaspoon turmeric, or to taste
¼ teaspoon garlic powder, or to taste
salt and pepper to taste, divided
1 small cabbage, shredded
¾-1 cup plain low-fat yogurt
1 tablespoon brown sugar

Remove and discard skin and fat from the chicken breast halves. Melt the margarine in a covered frying pan over medium heat.

Brown the chicken pieces on both sides. Sprinkle with the onions, 1/2 teaspoon of the paprika, the turmeric, the garlic powder, and the salt and pepper to taste.

Cover and cook the chicken pieces, turning once, for 20-25 minutes, or until well done and tender. Set aside and keep warm.

In a medium saucepan, combine the cabbage, ¾ cup of the yogurt, the remaining ½ teaspoon of paprika, and the sugar. Cover and cook over low heat for 15-20 minutes, adding more yogurt if necessary to prevent dryness.

Stir the cabbage mixture occasionally. When the cabbage is crisp-tender, check the seasonings and add the remaining salt and pepper to taste.

Remove the cabbage from the heat, turn into a serving dish, arrange the reserved chicken pieces on top, and serve.

CORNED BEEF AND CABBAGE

PREPARATION TIME: 15-20 MINUTES
COOKING TIME: 4 ½-5 HOURS
YIELD: 4-8 SERVINGS

4-5 pounds corned beef brisket
water
1 bay leaf
1 teaspoon ground thyme
½ teaspoon ground rosemary
2 small onions, quartered
1 small turnip, quartered
2 small kohlrabi, quartered
3 medium carrots, halved
3 medium potatoes, quartered
1 small cabbage, quartered and cored
salt and pepper to taste
assorted mustards

Though this recipe calls for only two pounds of corned beef brisket, we cook at least four pounds, reserving the extra for Russian Reubens *or* Molded Corned Beef and Cabbage Salad *(see pages 86, 81).*

Cover the meat with the water in a large covered saucepan. Add the bay leaf, the thyme, and the rosemary. Cook, covered, for 4 hours, or until the meat is fork tender, keeping covered with water. Remove when tender and set aside.

Return the water to a boil, add the onions, the turnip, the kohlrabi, and the carrots and cook until crisp-tender. Add the potatoes and the cabbage and cook until just tender.

Check the seasonings and add the salt and pepper to taste. Reduce the heat to low.

Cut off all but 2 pounds of the reserved meat and set the extra aside. Return the 2 pounds of meat to the vegetable mixture in the saucepan. Let simmer until piping hot.

Ladle some of the broth into a gravy boat or pitcher. Remove the meat, cut into thin slices, and arrange on a platter. Arrange the vegetables around the sliced meat.

Serve with broth and the assorted mustards on the side.

MORE-THAN-JUST-MEAT LOAF

PREPARATION TIME: 15-20 MINUTES
BAKING TIME: 60-75 MINUTES
YIELD: 6-8 SERVINGS

1 egg
½-¾ cup milk
2 slices bread, cubed
¼ teaspoon celery seed
¼ teaspoon thyme
¼ teaspoon ground sage
½ teaspoon dry mustard
dash garlic powder
salt and pepper to taste
1 ½ cups cooked grated carrots
½ cup minced onions
1 ½ pounds lean ground beef
8-10 saltine crackers, crushed and
    divided
1 ½ cups cooked chopped kale

Kale and carrots make this meat loaf worth its weight in nutritional gold. Both are bursting with beta-carotene and the kale is also rich in vitamin C.

Preheat the oven to 375° F. Have ready a 9 5/8-inch loaf pan.

In a large mixing bowl, whisk the egg and ½ cup of the milk. Stir in the bread cubes and let soften. Add the celery seed, the thyme, the sage, the mustard, the garlic powder, and the salt and pepper. Stir in the carrots and the onions, blending well.

Work the ground beef through the carrot mixture with your hands to ensure an even texture, adding more milk if too stiff.

Form half the meat mixture into a ball, roll in the crushed crackers, and flatten into the loaf pan. Spread with the kale.

Make a ball of the remaining meat mixture, roll in the crushed crackers, and shape to fit over the kale. Sprinkle with any remaining crushed crackers.

Bake the meat loaf for 60-75 minutes, or until well done. Remove from the oven and pour off and discard accumulated fat.

Let the meat loaf stand for 10 minutes. Loosen around the sides with a spatula, invert over a serving platter, and ease out carefully, loosening with the spatula. Serve.

CORNISH HENS AND BRUSSELS SPROUTS

PREPARATION TIME: 60-75 MINUTES
YIELD: 4 SERVINGS

When we are having guests we want to honor with a fine meal—and impress with our culinary savoir faire—*we give them* Cornish Hens and Brussels Sprouts. *Unusual and elegant, the dish is well worth the time it takes to prepare.*

1 tablespoon canola oil
1 small onion, minced
¾ cup white chablis
¼ teaspoon tarragon leaves
⅛ teaspoon cayenne pepper
1 tablespoon Worcestershire sauce
1 tablespoon lemon juice
4 Cornish game hens
salt and pepper to taste, divided
water
Spicy Apple Jelly Sauce
   (see opposite page)
20 ounces Brussels sprouts
⅓ cup soft margarine
2 cups cooked brown rice
¼ cup minced parsley

Preheat the oven to 375° F. Have ready a shallow roasting pan with rack.

Heat the oil in a medium saucepan and sauté the onion until limp. Add the chablis, the tarragon, the cayenne pepper, the Worcestershire sauce, and the lemon juice. Simmer, uncovered, for 5 minutes. Set aside.

Remove the giblets and necks from the body cavities of the hens. Set aside. Dust cavities with the salt and pepper to taste.

Truss legs and wings of the hens. Place on roasting pan rack and roast, uncovered, for 40-60 minutes, or until well done. Baste frequently with the reserved lemon juice mixture.

Place the reserved giblets and necks in a small saucepan with 1 cup of water and a pinch of salt and pepper, or to taste. Cook, covered, for 15-20 minutes, or until well done. Drain. Reserve the stock and set aside. Reserve the giblets and necks for some other use.

Prepare *Spicy Apple Jelly Sauce* (see opposite page). Set aside and keep warm.

About 15 minutes before hens are done, combine accumulated pan and basting juices with ½ cup of the reserved giblet stock and water to make 1 cup. Bring to a boil in a medium covered saucepan. Add the sprouts, and salt to taste. Cover and cook until crisp-tender. Drain, set aside, and keep warm.

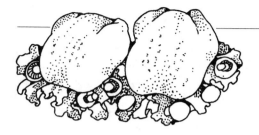

Melt the margarine in a medium frying pan and sauté the rice for 10-15 minutes, stirring constantly, until heated through and golden brown. Stir in the parsley. Set aside and keep warm.

Remove the hens from the oven. Spread the reserved rice on a serving platter and arrange the hens on it, with the reserved Brussels sprouts in a ring around the hens.

Serve with individual small dishes or cups of *Spicy Apple Jelly Sauce* on the side for dipping morsels of the roast fowl.

SPICY APPLE JELLY SAUCE

PREPARATION TIME: 10-15 MINUTES
YIELD: ABOUT 1 CUP

1 ¼ cups cream sherry
2 whole cloves
¹/₈ teaspoon nutmeg
¹/₈ teaspoon allspice
¹/₈ teaspoon thyme
½ teaspoon grated lemon zest
¼ cup giblet stock
⅓ cup apple jelly
⅓ cup orange juice
1 tablespoon soft margarine

Combine the sherry, the cloves, the nutmeg, the allspice, the thyme, and the lemon zest in a small saucepan. Bring to a boil and cook until reduced by one-half.

Add the giblet stock, the jelly, the orange juice, and the margarine. Stir until the jelly is melted.

Remove the cloves, pour the *Sauce* into small dishes or cups, and serve.

SWEDISH MEATBALL CABBAGE

PREPARATION TIME: 30-35 MINUTES
BAKING TIME: 2-3 HOURS
YIELD: 4-6 SERVINGS

Even in southern Sweden where many of our family originated, it is easier to grow the "winter" vegetables that comprise BROCCOLI & COMPANY, than "summer" vegetables that require hot days and warm nights. This dish, featuring sturdy cabbage, nutritious brown rice, and the leanest ground beef, is one of our all-time favorites. With it we serve side dishes of sour cream and a steaming casserole of Mother's Scalloped Potatoes. Together, they make up a world class meal that can be prepared and popped into the oven to bake while you do other things.

1 large cabbage, whole
1 6-ounce can tomato sauce
¼ cup lemon juice
1 cup beef broth
4 teaspoons sugar
1 pound extra-lean ground beef
1 egg, beaten
½ cup low-fat milk
⅔ cup cooked brown rice
salt and pepper to taste
sour cream
Mother's Scalloped Potatoes
   (see opposite page)

Preheat the oven to 375° F. Lightly oil a deep 2–3-quart covered nonmetal baking or casserole dish.

Blanch the cabbage in boiling water to cover in a large saucepan for 10-15 minutes, or until somewhat limp. Drain and set aside to cool.

Combine the tomato sauce, the lemon juice, the broth, and the sugar in a small mixing bowl. Set aside.

In a large mixing bowl, thoroughly blend the meat, the egg, the milk, the rice, and the salt and pepper to taste. Set aside.

Cut out and discard the core of the reserved cabbage. Carefully peel off 6-8 of the largest outer leaves. Set aside.

Place the cabbage head upside down in the center of the prepared baking dish. Place your hands back to back in the cavity left by the discarded core and spread the cabbage, loosening interlocking leaves gently from the center outward to form a large cup. Spread to cover sides and bottom of the dish evenly.

Turn the reserved meat mixture into the cabbage cup and arrange the reserved outer leaves over the top, tucking down around the sides to form a neat meat-filled ball.

Pour the reserved tomato sauce mixture over the ball, cover, and bake for 2-3 hours, or until tender and well done. Serve with a dish of sour cream on the side and *Mother's Scalloped Potatoes*.

MOTHER'S SCALLOPED POTATOES

PREPARATION TIME: 15-20 MINUTES
BAKING TIME: 1-1 ½ HOURS
YIELD: 4-6 SERVINGS

4 medium unblemished russet
  potatoes
1 medium onion, thinly sliced
4 tablespoons all-purpose flour
¾ teaspoon prepared mustard
5 tablespoons soft margarine or
  butter, divided
1 ½-2 cups whole milk
1 teaspoon salt, or to taste
freshly ground black pepper to taste

This potato casserole dish is a perfect companion for our sturdy, straightforward Swedish Meatball Cabbage. *Prepare and put it in to bake about an hour and a half before the meat dish is ready so that both can come to the table piping hot.*

Preheat the oven to 375° F. Have ready a lightly oiled 2–3-quart covered nonmetal baking dish.

Scrub the potatoes clean and cut into thin slices in a large mixing bowl. Add the onion slices and sprinkle the mixture with the flour, tossing to coat evenly. Turn into the prepared baking dish.

Blend the mustard into the margarine or butter and dot the surface of the potato mixture. Set aside.

Heat the milk to just under a boil, stir in the salt and pepper, and pour over the reserved potato mixture so the liquid reaches the top layer but does not cover it. Set any remaining milk aside to be added later if needed to keep potatoes moist.

Cover the baking dish, place in the oven, and bake for 1-1 ½ hours, or until tender, removing the cover for the final half hour. Serve.

GOLDEN DELICIOUS CASSEROLE

PREPARATION TIME: 45-60 MINUTES
YIELD: 4 SERVINGS

1 tablespoon canola oil
4 chicken breast halves, skin and fat
  removed
½ cup minced green onions
1 small cabbage, shredded
2 Golden Delicious apples, peeled,
  cored, and quartered
1 teaspoon grated fresh gingerroot
⅛ cup molasses
½ cup water
1 tablespoon lemon juice
salt and pepper to taste

Preheat the oven to 375° F. Have ready a covered 2-quart casserole dish.

Heat the oil in a medium frying pan and brown the chicken pieces on both sides. Remove and set aside.

Sauté the onions and the cabbage in the remaining oil for 5 minutes. Remove from the heat and turn half the cabbage mixture into the casserole, arrange the chicken and the apple quarters on top, and add the other half of the cabbage.

Combine the gingerroot, the molasses, the water, the lemon juice, and the salt and pepper in the frying pan and stir until well mixed. Pour over the cabbage mixture.

Cover the casserole and bake for 20-30 minutes, or until the chicken is well done.

Remove from the oven and serve.

MEAL-IN-ONE

PREPARATION TIME: 15-20 MINUTES
COOKING TIME: 1 ½-2 HOURS
YIELD: 4 SERVINGS

¾ pound extra-lean lamb, cubed
1 small onion, minced
1 small cabbage, shredded
1 ½ tablespoons all-purpose flour,
  divided
salt and pepper to taste
2 medium potatoes, peeled and
  quartered
½-1 cup water

This is the kind of meal we favor: Cooked in one pot—protein, carbohydrates, vitamins, and fiber—perfectly simple to make and perfectly wonderful to eat.

Brown the meat in a heavy covered saucepan over medium-high heat. Remove and set aside.

Sauté the onion until limp. Remove and set aside. Turn the heat to low.

Put half the cabbage in the saucepan. Sprinkle with ½ tablespoon of the flour and a little salt and pepper.

Layer the reserved meat, the reserved onions, and the potatoes over the cabbage and sprinkle with another ½ tablespoon of the flour. Put the remaining cabbage on top, sprinkle with the remaining flour, and a little more salt and pepper.

Add ½ cup of the water, cover the saucepan tightly, and simmer for 1 ½-2 hours, or until the meat and the vegetables are melt-in-the-mouth tender, adding more water if too dry.

Remove from the heat and serve.

CHEESY SALMON BAKE

PREPARATION TIME: 15-20 MINUTES
BAKING TIME: 30-35 MINUTES
YIELD: 4-6 SERVINGS

1 ½ cups cauliflowerets
1 ½ cups broccoli pieces
1 ½ tablespoons canola oil
2 green onions, minced
2 tablespoons all-purpose flour
1 ½ cups low-fat milk
¾ cup grated low-fat cheese
½ cup mushroom pieces
2 tablespoons lemon juice
½ teaspoon crushed dill seed
1 tablespoon minced parsley
1 7 ¾-ounce can salmon, drained
¼ cup grated Parmesan cheese

Nutritionists tell us that salmon is one of the best forms of protein we can eat: The little fat it contains helps lower blood cholesterol levels. We confess, however, that we have this dish often because of its taste, not because of its health benefits!

Preheat the oven to 350° F. Have ready a 2–3-quart casserole.

Cook the cauliflowerets and the broccoli pieces separately in as little water as possible until crisp-tender. Set aside.

Heat the oil in a large saucepan and sauté the onions until limp. Remove and set aside.

Stir the flour into the oil and cook until bubbly. Add the milk and cook until thick, stirring constantly to prevent lumps. Add the low-fat cheese, the mushroom pieces, the lemon juice, the dill seed, and the parsley to the flour mixture. Stir until the cheese is melted.

Drain the salmon and separate into chunks, removing bones and skin. Fold the salmon chunks, the reserved cauliflowerets and broccoli pieces, and the reserved onions through the cheese mixture.

Turn the salmon mixture into the casserole, sprinkle with the Parmesan cheese, and bake, uncovered, for 30-35 minutes, or until the mixture is bubbling and a cheesy crust has formed on the top.

Remove from the oven and serve.

CAULIFLOWER AND BEEF ORIENTAL

PREPARATION TIME: 10-15 MINUTES
YIELD: 4-6 SERVINGS

1 pound extra-lean flank or round
   steak
2 tablespoons cornstarch
1 tablespoon soy sauce
½ cup water
1 tablespoon dry sherry
½ tablespoon canola oil
1 small onion, thinly sliced
½ clove garlic, minced
1 cup beef bouillon
10 ounces cauliflowerets
1 cup snow peas
½ cup bean sprouts
½ cup sliced bamboo shoots
salt to taste

Timing is almost everything in stir-fry cooking. Have the ingredients measured, cut, mixed, or drained before you start to heat the frying pan or wok so there is no danger of overcooking the thin morsels of meat or the delicate fresh vegetables.

Slice the beef across the grain into narrow strips 1 ½ inches long. Set aside.

Combine the cornstarch, the soy sauce, the water, and the sherry in a small mixing bowl. Set aside.

Heat the oil to 375° F. in a large frying pan or wok. Add the reserved beef strips and cook until brown on all sides, stirring constantly. Add the onion and the garlic and cook 1 minute, stirring constantly.

Add the bouillon, the cauliflowerets, the peas, the bean sprouts, the bamboo shoots, and the salt to taste.

Cover and cook, stirring occasionally, for 5 minutes, or until vegetables are crisp-tender.

Stir the reserved soy sauce mixture and add to the beef mixture, stirring constantly. Cook until clear and slightly thick.

Remove from the heat, turn into a serving dish, and serve.

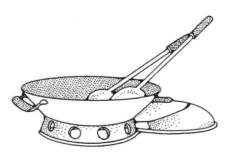

SURKAL MED POTATIS KORV

PREPARATION TIME: 45-60 MINUTES
YIELD: 4-6 SERVINGS

Our Swedish ancestors used to pack Potatis Korv *(Potato Sausage) into casings like those used for Polish and Italian varieties. Lacking the know-how, tools, and time to do things the old-fashioned way, we simply shape the meat and potato mixture into patties and fry or broil, as if they were made of ground beef.*

2 tablespoons canola oil, divided
1 medium onion, minced and divided
2 cups drained sauerkraut
1 tart apple, peeled, cored, and
  quartered
1/2 teaspoon ground caraway seed
2 medium-large potatoes
1/2 pound extra-lean ground beef
1/4 pound extra-lean ground pork
1/8 cup cooked brown rice
2 tablespoons beef broth
1/2 teaspoon ground sage
salt and pepper to taste

Heat 1 tablespoon of the oil in a large covered frying pan over medium heat and sauté half the onion until limp. Add the sauerkraut, the apple, and the caraway. Turn the heat to low and cover the pan.

Shred or grate the potatoes into a large mixing bowl. Add the remaining onion, the beef, the pork, the rice, the broth, the sage, and the salt and pepper to taste. Make a meat loaf-like mixture and shape into patties.

Heat the remaining oil in another frying pan and cook the patties, turning once, until browned and very well done.

Remove the patties from the frying pan and drain on paper towels.

Place the patties on the sauerkraut mixture, cover, and cook for another 15 minutes.

Turn the sauerkraut mixture onto a platter, arrange the patties around it, and serve.

BROCCOLI HAM BAKE

PREPARATION TIME: 15-20 MINUTES
BAKING TIME: 35-40 MINUTES
YIELD: 4-6 SERVINGS

1 egg
1 ¼ cups sour cream
¼ cup plain low-fat yogurt
2 green onions, minced
1 ½ teaspoons paprika, or to taste
salt to taste
water
16 ounces broccoli florets, divided
½ cup grated cheddar cheese, divided
2 cups cooked coarsely chopped ham,
    divided
¼ cup grated Parmesan cheese

Though the broccoli for this superb entrée should be freshly cooked when combined with the ham, the other ingredients can be prepared ahead of time and added just before popping the dish into the oven.

Preheat the oven to 375° F. Oil a 2-quart ovenproof dish.

In a medium mixing bowl, beat the egg with the sour cream and the yogurt until smooth. Stir in the onions, the paprika, and the salt. Set aside.

Cook the broccoli in a small amount of water in a medium covered saucepan until crisp-tender. Drain.

Place half of the broccoli in the prepared dish and cover with half of the cheddar cheese and half of the ham.

Arrange the remaining broccoli, cheddar cheese, and ham in alternating layers as above.

Pour the sour cream mixture over the broccoli mixture and sprinkle with the Parmesan cheese.

Bake for 35-40 minutes, or until brown on top and bubbly. Remove from the oven and serve.

COUSCOUS A LA DIANE

PREPARATION TIME: 15-20 MINUTES
COOKING TIME: AT LEAST 2 HOURS
YIELD: 4-8 SERVINGS

1 pound lamb stew meat, trimmed
   and cubed
½-1 small clove garlic, finely minced
4 tablespoons all-purpose flour
4-6 cups beef or chicken broth
1 medium onion, minced
2 celery stalks, diced
1 small green bell pepper, diced
2 medium carrots, diced
1 medium turnip, diced
¼ teaspoon thyme, or to taste
¼ teaspoon oregano, or to taste
½ bay leaf
¼ teaspoon saffron, or to taste
pinch each ginger, cloves, nutmeg,
   and cinnamon, or to taste
pinch each coriander and fennel, or to
   taste
salt and pepper to taste
2 cups shredded cabbage
1 cup cauliflowerets
2 cups tomato pieces
1 15 ½-ounce can garbanzo beans,
   with liquid

Couscous is a North African dish based on lamb, vegetables, and a fine semolina cereal grain. It can be spicy and hot or mild and delicate, depending on how liberal you are with the seasonings. We have given amounts that suit us, with "to taste" for a range of flexibility.

Heat a large, heavy covered saucepan and sear the lamb cubes until brown on all sides. Add the garlic and the flour, and cook, stirring until brown. Add 4 cups of the broth, stirring to prevent lumps.

Add the onion, the celery, the green pepper, the carrots, the turnip, the thyme, the oregano, the bay leaf, the saffron, the ginger, the cloves, the nutmeg, the cinnamon, the coriander, the fennel, and the salt and pepper. Cover and simmer 60-75 minutes, or until very tender, stirring occasionally.

Add the cabbage, the cauliflowerets, the tomato pieces, and more broth if too thick. Cover and simmer 15-20 minutes, or until tender, stirring occasionally.

Remove the bay leaf and check the seasonings. Reduce the heat and keep warm.

Drain the garbanzo beans, reserving beans and liquid. Set both aside.

Make *Hot Sauce* by combining in a small saucepan, the reserved garbanzo bean liquid and enough cooking liquid from the lamb mixture to make 1 cup. Stir in ½ tablespoon cornstarch, 1 beef bouillon cube, 2 tablespoons tomato catsup, ½-¾ teaspoon paprika, ¼-½ teaspoon coriander, and ¼-1 teaspoon cayenne pepper, or to taste.

Bring to a boil and stir constantly until the bouillon cube is completely dissolved and the mixture is smooth and thick.

Continue to cook for 10 minutes, stirring occasionally. Reduce the heat and keep warm.

Hot Sauce
couscous

Prepare the couscous according to package directions. Turn the couscous onto a serving platter, spoon the reserved lamb mixture evenly over it, and top with the reserved garbanzo beans. Serve with the reserved *Hot Sauce* on the side.

KIM LEFFLER'S BROCCOLI CASSEROLE

PREPARATION TIME: 10-15 MINUTES
BAKING TIME: 40-45 MINUTES
YIELD: 8 SERVINGS

4 tablespoons soft margarine, divided
1 cup fine dry bread crumbs
2 tablespoons all-purpose flour
½ teaspoon salt, or to taste
¼ teaspoon pepper, or to taste
1 ¼ cups low-fat milk
2 tablespoons instant minced onions
3 ounces cream cheese, cubed
20 ounces broccoli pieces, cooked
1 cup sliced water chestnuts
2 cups cooked cubed chicken or turkey

This is our kind of entrée—substantial, elegant, and irresistibly delicious. What's more, it is wonderfully adaptable: Delete the crumb topping and use the creamed mixture as filling for a two-crust 10-inch main dish pie, or prepare without the chicken or turkey and serve as a side dish.

Preheat the oven to 350° F. Oil a 2–3-quart casserole dish.

Melt 2 tablespoons of the margarine in a small saucepan. Add the crumbs and stir over low heat until the margarine has been absorbed. Remove from the heat and set aside.

In a large saucepan, melt the remaining 2 tablespoons of margarine. Add the flour, the salt, and the pepper, and cook until bubbly.

Add the milk and the onions and cook until thick, stirring constantly to prevent lumps.

Stir in the cream cheese until melted. Fold in the broccoli pieces, the water chestnuts, and the chicken or turkey.

Turn into the prepared casserole. Top with the reserved bread crumb mixture and bake for 40 minutes, or until bubbly and lightly brown.

Remove from the oven and serve.

BEIJING-STYLE STIR-FRY

PREPARATION TIME: 40-45 MINUTES
YIELD: 4-6 SERVINGS

1 cup chicken broth
1 ounce dried black mushrooms
  (Shiitake)
canola oil
2 chicken breasts, skinned, boned,
  and cut into ½-inch strips
1 small green bell pepper, julienned
1 cup broccoli pieces
2 small zucchini, sliced into thin
  rounds
6 green onions, cut into 2-inch strips
½ small cabbage, coarsely chopped
1 cup snow peas
½ tablespoon cornstarch
½ teaspoon ground ginger, or to taste
dash garlic powder, or to taste
2 tablespoons dry sherry
1 ½ tablespoons soy sauce
1 cup salted peanuts

Bring the broth to a boil in a small saucepan, add the mushrooms, remove from the heat, and let stand for 30 minutes. Drain, reserving the mushrooms and the cooking liquid. Discard the mushroom stems. Chop the mushroom caps coarsely. Set aside.

Heat ½ tablespoon of the oil in a large frying pan or wok and sauté the chicken strips in small batches until cooked through. Remove and keep warm.

Add more oil if necessary and when heated, sauté the pepper, the broccoli, the zucchini, and the onions for 3 minutes, stirring constantly. Add the cabbage and the snow peas. Stir and cook for 5-10 minutes. Remove and keep warm.

Stir the cornstarch into the reserved mushroom liquid. Add the ginger, the garlic powder, the sherry, and the soy sauce. Turn into the pan or wok and cook, stirring constantly, for 1 minute or until thick.

Stir the reserved mushrooms and the reserved cabbage mixture into the soy sauce mixture until coated. Turn off the heat.

Arrange the reserved chicken strips on a large serving platter, cover with the cabbage mixture, and sprinkle with the peanuts. Serve.

ODDS & ENDS

To make a Cabbage-Lettuce Pye: Take some of the largest and hardest cabbage-lettuce you can get; boil them in salt and water till they are tender; then lay them in a colander to drain dry; then have your paste laid in your pattipan ready, and lay butter on the bottom; then lay in your lettuce and some artichoke-bottoms, and some large pieces of marrow, and the yolks of eight hard eggs, and some scalded sorrel; bake it, and when it comes out of the oven, cut open the lid; and pour in a caudle made with white-wine and sugar, and thickened with eggs; so serve it hot. Old Cookery Books and Ancient Cuisine

—W. Carew Hazlitt, London, 1902

MOTHER'S GREEN CABBAGE AND TOMATO RELISH

PREPARATION TIME: 15-20 MINUTES
STANDING TIME: 12 HOURS OR
  OVERNIGHT
COOKING TIME: 30-45 MINUTES
PROCESSING TIME: 5 MINUTES (SEE
  PAGE 125)
YIELD: 3-4 PINTS

4 cups chopped green tomatoes
1 cup chopped sweet red pepper
1 cup chopped green pepper
1 ½ cups chopped onions
5 cups (about 2 pounds) chopped
  cabbage
⅓ cup pure granulated uniodized salt
3 cups cider or white vinegar (4-6
  percent acidity)
2 cups brown sugar, packed
2 tablespoons whole mixed pickling
  spice

Mother used to make relish at harvest time, following a recipe she probably got from her mother. Basically, it is identical to one included in USDA Home & Garden Bulletin No. 92, so we have given amounts and directions from there. Though at first glance it would seem to be more bother than it's worth to make pickles, most of the work is done once the vegetables are chopped.

Prepare four pint jars and lids. Use jars and lids free of cracks, chips, rust, dents, or any defect that may prevent airtight seals and cause spoilage. Select the size of lid—wide mouth or regular—that fits jars which are specifically designed for home canning. Other jars may break more easily or not seal properly. Wash jars in hot, soapy water. Rinse thoroughly with hot water. If two-piece lids are used, wash and rinse flat metal lids and metal screw bands. Always use **new** flat metal lids. They may have to be boiled or held in boiling water for a few minutes before they are used. Follow manufacturer's directions. For porcelain-lined zinc caps, use clean, new rubber rings of the right size for the jars. Do not test by stretching. Dip rubber rings in boiling water before putting them on the jars. Set jars and lids aside.

Have ready a water-bath canner deep enough to allow for 1 or 2 inches of water above the tops of the jars, plus a little extra space for boiling. It should have a close-fitting cover and be equipped with a wire or wood rack with partitions to keep jars from touching each other and falling against the sides of the canner.

Combine the tomatoes, the peppers, the onions, and the cabbage with the salt in a large glass or china container and let stand 12 hours or overnight. Drain and press in a clean, thin, white cloth to remove all the liquid possible. Discard the liquid.

In a large stainless steel, enamelware, or glass saucepan, blend the vinegar and the sugar. Bring to a boil.

Place the pickling spice mixture loosely in a clean cloth and tie with a string. Add to the vinegar mixture.

Bring water in the canner to a boil.

Place reserved jars and lids in a large saucepan with water to cover and bring to a boil.

Add the reserved cabbage mixture to the vinegar mixture, return to a boil, and cook gently, stirring occasionally, for about 30 minutes, or until reduced one-half in volume. Remove spice bag.

Pack the cabbage mixture into the reserved jars, filling to ½ inch from tops. Adjust the lids according to manufacturer's directions.

Immerse jars in the boiling water in the canner so there are 1 or 2 inches of water above their tops. Add boiling water if necessary, but do not pour directly on jars or lids.

Cover canner and bring water back to a boil as quickly as possible. Start to count processing time as soon as the water in the canner returns to a boil.

Boil gently and steadily for 5 minutes or more, depending on the altitude where you live (see page 125).

Remove jars immediately and seal lids as directed by manufacturer. Set jars upright several inches apart on a wire rack or folded towel to cool for 12-24 hours.

Check lids for airtight seal as directed by manufacturer. If properly sealed, label jars and store in a dark, cool, dry place where there is no danger of freezing.

If improperly sealed, use *Relish* right away, or recan. To recan, empty the jar, repack in a clean sterilized jar with a **new**, clean, sterilized lid, and reprocess as before.

SAUERKRAUT CHOCOLATE CAKE

PREPARATION TIME: 15-20 MINUTES
BAKING TIME: 25-30 MINUTES
YIELD: ONE 9 BY 9
   OR 11 BY 7-INCH CAKE

We were as surprised as you must be, when we saw this recipe of Cousin Mary's for the first time. Sauerkraut cake? Sauerkraut chocolate cake? "Really, Cousin Mary!" we muttered under our breath. Nevertheless, for the sake of family relations, we said nothing aloud, smiled bravely, and tried the cake. It's a winner! Literally. You can give odds against anyone's guessing the ingredients, even after they have eaten the whole cake—which they will, if you let them. We'll give odds on that!

⅔ cup margarine
1 ⅓ cups sugar
3 eggs
1 teaspoon pure vanilla extract
1 cup water
2 ¼ cups all-purpose flour
1 teaspoon baking powder
1 teaspoon baking soda
½ cup cocoa
⅔ cup drained finely chopped
   sauerkraut
Cocoa Frosting (see below)

Preheat the oven to 350° F. Oil and flour a 9 by 9- or 11 by 7-inch baking pan.

In a large mixing bowl, cream together the margarine and the sugar. Beat in the eggs, the vanilla, and the water.

Add the flour, the baking powder, the baking soda, the cocoa, and the salt and beat to a smooth batter. Stir in the sauerkraut until thoroughly blended.

Turn the sauerkraut mixture into the prepared pan and bake for 25-30 minutes, or until a tester inserted in the center comes out clean.

Remove from the oven and cool on a rack.

When the cake is completely cool, spread with the *Cocoa Frosting*, cut into portions, and serve.

COCOA FROSTING
PREPARATION TIME: 5-10 MINUTES
YIELD: ABOUT 1 CUP

3 tablespoons soft margarine
¼ cup cocoa
1 ½ cups powdered sugar
½ teaspoon pure vanilla extract
2-4 tablespoons milk

In a medium mixing bowl, cream the margarine and the cocoa. Add the powdered sugar, the vanilla, and enough of the milk to make the mixture of spreading consistency.

Beat until smooth and creamy. Spread on cooled cake.

RUTABAGA PUDDING

PREPARATION TIME: 25-30 MINUTES
YIELD: 4-6 SERVINGS

1 ½ cups cooked pureed rutabagas
1 ½ cups evaporated milk
3 eggs, slightly beaten
1 teaspoon pure lemon extract
½ cup molasses
½ cup brown sugar, packed
¼ cup granulated sugar
½ teaspoon salt
1 teaspoon cinnamon
½ teaspoon ginger
½ teaspoon nutmeg
¼ teaspoon cloves
Rum Butter Sauce (see below)

Down-to-earth rutabagas are usually regarded as too plebeian to be considered for use in a dessert dish, but we are here to testify that ''swedes'' can be sweet when they want to. Witness this pudding.

In a large mixing bowl, combine the rutabagas, the milk, the eggs, the lemon extract, and the molasses, and beat until smooth. Add the brown sugar, the granulated sugar, the salt, the cinnamon, the ginger, the nutmeg, and the cloves, blending well.

Turn into a double boiler over hot water and cook until thick, stirring occasionally to prevent lumps. Turn the heat to low and keep warm while preparing the *Rum Butter Sauce*, below.

RUM BUTTER SAUCE
PREPARATION TIME: 10-20 MINUTES
YIELD: ABOUT 1 CUP

¾ cup sugar
½ cup butter or soft margarine
½ cup half-and-half
dark rum or pure rum extract

In a medium saucepan, combine the sugar, the butter or margarine, and the half-and-half. Bring to just under a boil, reduce the heat to low, and cook, stirring occasionally, until smooth and slightly thick. Stir in the dark rum or rum extract to taste. Remove from the heat and serve with *Rutabaga Pudding*.

HAUSKRAUT

PREPARATION TIME: 45-60 MINUTES
STANDING TIME: 3 WEEKS
PROCESSING TIME: 15 MINUTES
   (SEE PAGE 125)
YIELD: 7-8 PINTS

12 ½ pounds firm mature cabbage
⅓ cup plus 1 ½ tablespoons pure
  granulated uniodized salt

HOW TO MAKE SAUERKRAUT
(See USDA Home and Garden Bulletin No. 92
pages 25-28.)

1. **Remove the outer leaves from firm, mature
   heads of cabbage; discard. Wash and
   drain remaining cabbage. Remove core.**

"Hauskraut" means homemade sauerkraut, distinctly different from commercially processed varieties. The directions that follow are generic, coming from the U.S. Department of Agriculture. The recipe can be halved or doubled, as long as the proportions remain the same.

Prepare eight pint jars and lids. Use jars and lids free of cracks, chips, rust, dents, or any defect that may prevent airtight seals and cause spoilage. Select the size of lid—wide mouth or regular—that fits jars which are specifically designed for home canning. Other jars may break more easily or not seal properly. Wash jars in hot, soapy water. Rinse thoroughly with hot water. If two-piece lids are used, wash and rinse flat metal lids and metal screw bands. Always use **new** flat metal lids. They may have to be boiled or held in boiling water for a few minutes before they are used. Follow manufacturer's directions. For porcelain-lined zinc caps, use clean, new rubber rings of the right size for the jars. Do not test by stretching. Dip rubber rings in boiling water before putting them on the jars. Set jars and lids aside.

Have ready a clean, sterilized 1 ½-2 gallon stone crock or glass jar and two large heavy-duty plastic bags suitable for food storage, which can be sealed watertight. Set aside.

Have ready a water-bath canner deep enough to allow for 1 or 2 inches of water above the tops of the jars, plus a little extra space for boiling. The canner should have a close-fitting cover and a wire or wood rack with partitions to keep jars from touching each other and falling against the sides of the canner. Set aside.

Remove and discard outer leaves and any undesirable portions from the cabbage. Wash and drain remaining cabbage. Cut into

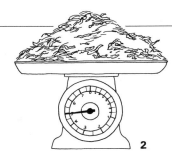

2. Shred cabbage and weigh 5 pounds. Accuracy in weighing is important to insure correct proportion of cabbage to salt.

3. Measure 3 tablespoons pure granulated salt and sprinkle over 5 pounds shredded cabbage.

Allow the salted cabbage to stand a few minutes to wilt slightly. Mix well, with clean hands or a spoon, to distribute salt uniformly.

halves or quarters; remove cores. Use a shredder or sharp knife to cut the cabbage into thin shreds, about the thickness of a dime.

In a large enamelware, glass, or stainless steel container, thoroughly mix 3 tablespoons salt with 5 pounds shredded cabbage. Let stand for several minutes to wilt slightly; this allows packing without excessive breaking or bruising of the shreds.

Pack firmly and evenly into a clean stone crock or glass jar. Using a wooden spoon, a tamper, or your hands, press down firmly until juice comes to surface. Repeat the shredding, salting, and packing of the cabbage until used up and/or until the crock is filled to within no more than 3 or 4 inches from the top.

Fill one reserved plastic bag with water and seal. *The bag should be of heavyweight, watertight plastic, and intended for use with food.* It should be filled with enough water to form a tightfitting cover over the cabbage in order to keep out air and prevent the growth of yeast or mold.

Tie the plastic bag tightly so the water will not leak out. For added protection, place the first waterfilled bag inside another heavyweight, watertight plastic bag intended for food use. Check bags daily for leaks. If a small amount of water leaks out, it will not hurt the cabbage, but the bag should be replaced.

Store the crock or jar of cabbage at room temperature (68° to 72° F.) for 3 weeks while fermenting.

Bring water in the canner to a boil.

Place reserved jars and lids in a shallow pan with an inch or two of water. Bring to just under a boil.

Turn the sauerkraut into a large stainless steel, enamelware, or glass saucepan and heat to simmering (185° to 210° F.). Do not boil.

Pack into reserved jars and cover with hot juice to ½ inch from top of jar. Adjust the lids as directed by manufacturer.

4. Pack the salted cabbage into container. Press firmly with wooden spoon, masher, or with hands until the juices drawn out just cover the shredded cabbage.

Immerse filled, sealed jars in the water in the canner. Add boiling water if necessary to reach 1 to 2 inches above the tops of the jars, but do not pour directly on jars or lids.

Cover and bring water back to a boil as quickly as possible. Start to count processing time when the water returns to a boil. Boil gently and steadily for 15 minutes (see page 125).

Remove jars immediately and complete lid seals if necessary. Set jars upright several inches apart on a wire rack or a folded towel to cool for 12-24 hours.

Check lids for airtight seal as directed by manufacturer. If properly sealed, label jars and store in a dark, cool, dry place where there is no danger of freezing.

If improperly sealed, use *Hauskraut* right away, or recan. To recan, empty the jar, repack in a clean sterilized jar with a **new**, clean, sterilized lid, and reprocess as before.

Making Pickles and Relishes at Home, Home and Garden Bulletin No. 92 can be obtained through your local extension service office. It includes information on common causes of spoilage in sauerkraut:

Soft kraut: Softness in sauerkraut may result from insufficient salt, too high temperatures during fermentation, uneven distribution of salt, or air pockets caused by improper packing.

Pink kraut: Pink color in kraut is caused by growth of certain types of yeast on the surface of the kraut. These may grow if there is too much salt, an uneven distribution of salt, or if the kraut is improperly covered or weighted during fermentation.

Rotted kraut: This condition in kraut is usually found at the surface where the cabbage has not been covered sufficiently to exclude air during fermentation.

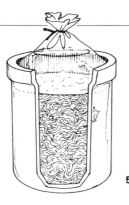

5

5. Place a water-filled plastic bag on top of the cabbage. A water-filled plastic bag fits snugly against the cabbage and against the sides of the container and prevents exposure to air.

6. After three weeks, remove from container and heat in kettle to simmering temperature. Pack hot sauerkraut into clean, hot jars; cover with hot juice, filling to ½ inch from top of jar. Adjust lids. Place jars in boiling-water bath and process 15 minutes for pints and 20 minutes for quarts. Start to count the processing time as soon as hot jars are placed in the actively boiling water.

7. Remove jars from the canner and complete seals if necessary. Set jars upright on a wire rack or folded towel to cool. Place them several inches apart.

Dark kraut: Darkness in kraut may be caused by unwashed and improperly trimmed cabbage, insufficient juice to cover fermenting cabbage, uneven distribution of salt, exposure to air, high temperatures during fermentation, processing and storage, or long storage.

Note: Processing time is given for altitudes less than 1000 feet above sea level. At 1000 feet or above, increase recommended processing times by one minute for each additional 1000 feet of altitude.

6

7

GRANDMOTHER'S BREAD STUFFING

PREPARATION TIME: 15-20 MINUTES
YIELD: 4-6 SERVINGS

¼ cup soft margarine or butter
1 medium onion, minced
1 tablespoon minced parsley
1 cup cooked minced kale
½-1 cup beef or chicken broth
7-8 slices week-old whole wheat
  bread
¼ teaspoon salt, or to taste
dash pepper
½ teaspoon thyme
⅛ teaspoon rosemary
½ teaspoon ground sage

Melt the margarine or butter in a medium saucepan and sauté the onion and the parsley until limp. Stir in the kale. Turn the heat to low.

Heat the broth in a small saucepan to just under a boil.

Tear the bread into bite-size pieces and add to the kale mixture. Sprinkle with the salt, the pepper, the thyme, the rosemary, and the sage. Mix well.

Stir in enough broth to moisten the bread mixture to your taste.

Serve at once as a side dish, or use the mixture to stuff chops or fowl.

GROWING & HARVESTING

Pangloss sometimes said to Candide: "All events are linked together in the best of all possible worlds; for after all, if you had not been expelled from a fine castle . . . for love of Mademoiselle Cunegonde, if you had not been subjected to the Inquisition, if you had not traveled about America on foot, if you had not given the Baron a great blow with your sword, if you had not lost all your sheep from the good country of Eldorado, you would not be here eating candied citrons and pistachios." "That is well said," replied Candide, "but we must cultivate our garden."

—Voltaire

BROCCOLI & COMPANY vegetables are cool-season plants with higher food value per pound and per square foot than warm-season crops since the *vegetative* part—not the fruit—of the cool-season plant is eaten: the *roots* of turnip and rutabaga; the *leaves* of cabbage, kale, Brussels sprouts, collards, and mustard greens; and the *immature flower parts* of broccoli and cauliflower. Though the plants differ in appearance, strong *Brassica* family genes are present, and the same good practices of gardening apply to all.

It is best to plan on paper before planting in the garden. Make a sketch showing dimensions of the garden area. List kinds and amounts of vegetables to be planted, location for each vegetable, and spacing between plants and rows. Schedule dates of spring and fall plantings. (See page *135.*)

Most cruciferous plants prefer cool to cold weather, especially when maturing. They do best at temperatures of 60–65° F. during the growing period. Seeds are tiny, with one ounce of cabbage seed, for example, producing as many as 2000 plants.

Fertilize the planting bed or garden plot well ahead of the time you plant seeds or transplant seedlings to the outdoors. *Cruciferae* can be grown in a wide range of soils, but fertile, deep, well-drained sandy and silt loams are best. Beds are recommended for rutabagas and turnips, made by building soil level up 4-6 inches and wide enough to accommodate the number of rows you want. This arrangement makes it easier for roots to expand and grow. Soil should be rich in nitrogen,

phosphorous, and potassium, but low in alkali. If you are uncertain about the composition of the soil in your garden plot, have it analyzed by the nearest extension service office of the U.S. Department of Agriculture. Apply nutrients and/or fertilizer as directed for specific varieties.

Plow, spade, or rototill the soil to loosen and oxygenate. Work to a depth of at least 6 inches. Break large clods with a spading fork or rake to pea-sized granules.

Seeds can be germinated and seedlings started in a box, pan, or flowerpot set in a window or other sunny location, as well as in a cold frame. Soil pellets—composed of a well-balanced synthetic mixture free of diseases and weeds—are the simplest and easiest method for starting plants and are available at most garden supply stores. Start the seedlings 5-7 weeks before outdoor planting dates recommended on seed packets. Put each plant into its own pot when 1-2 inches tall. Transplants are also available at most nurseries or garden centers.

Experts recommend fertilizing seedlings with plant food every ten days to two weeks until transplanting, beginning just after the first true leaves appear. Keep soil moist until the seeds have germinated. From that time on water generously, but make sure the planting bed is well drained.

Plants should be gradually hardened, or toughened before planting in the open by reducing growing temperature and water, withholding fertilizer, and increasing light intensity. Frequently this is done by placing the plants outside during favorable weather in the last two to three weeks before setting in the garden. Take the plants indoors if frost is expected. Water if the plants start to wilt.

Set the starts a bit deeper in the garden soil than they were in their pots. Leave space between rows and plants according to seed packet directions or see page 136.

When planting directly in the garden, sow seeds as early in the spring as the ground can be worked. Since *cruciferae* are relatively fast-starting, early spring planting will allow some—such as early cabbages—to mature before the hottest days of summer: Those that need a full growing season for maturation will be able to get a good start before hot weather slows them down. Second plantings for fall harvesting—or for wintering outdoors in mild latitudes—can be made during late spring or summer in garden space taken up earlier by spring crops such as lettuce, peas, or radishes.

Control weeds (and some pests) by spreading black plastic between rows, or mulching with lawn clippings, straw, or other natural materials. Some experts suggest putting protective paper mats around the base of each plant to keep worms away from tender stalks and leaves. Pull or hoe weeds when they first appear, being careful to avoid injuring vegetable roots that lie near the surface.

There are many natural means and methods of controlling the diseases and pests—such as clubroot, blackleg, yellows, black rot, various worms, aphids, slugs, nematodes, and beetles—that threaten *cruciferae*. Companion planting with marigolds, sage, catnip, thyme, and rosemary are said to protect these plants from many insects and nematodes. "Good bugs" and birds will take care of some pests. Worms and snails may be removed by hand; other insects may be washed off with a fine spray of water from a garden hose. Consult county extension service agents before using any chemical insecticides, and be *extremely* cautious in their use.

Crop rotation and sanitation in the garden area will help reduce damage from many insects and diseases. We are advised by experts to plant Broccoli & Company vegetables in a different part of our garden every year and to clean out and get rid of discarded roots and leaves at the end of the gardening season.

Harvest vegetables in the early morning when they are at their best for eating fresh, and store under conditions—either for short term or long term—to keep them that way as long as possible. (See page 14.)

BROCCOLI (*Brassica oleracea italica*)

The broccoli plant with which most of us are familiar is "sprouting" broccoli, as distinguished from "heading" broccoli, which is almost identical to cauliflower. One planting may produce for as long as three months because of production from axillary shoots. Transplants mature in 50-85 days. Maturity takes 65-100 days when seeded in the garden, depending on the time of year and variety planted. Planting with different maturities can extend the harvest season for a month or more, even through the first fall frost as long as buds are not developing when freezing occurs.

The immature dark green flower heads, parts of the attached small leaves, and a considerable portion—4-8 inches—of the stem of the broccoli plant are edible. They should be harvested before buds open.

Suggested varieties include: Calabrese, De Cicco, Green Comet, Green Duke, Green Goliath, Premium Crop, Spartan Early, Gem, Pacifica, Topper, and Waltham 29.

Seeds for a special variety called *broccoli raab* are also available. Italian in background like sprouting broccoli, raab is a wholly different plant, with no large central head. Stems are slender and heads numerous, button-size, loose, and open. The tender leaves are edible and are cooked together with the flower as greens. A delicacy not normally found in supermarket produce bins, raab is occasionally available at specialty produce markets.

BRUSSELS SPROUTS (*Brassica oleracea gemmifera*)

It's almost a truism that if you *like* cabbage, you'll *love* Brussels sprouts.

A biennial that produces sprouts the first year and seeds the second, sprouts need a long, cool growing season to thrive. Like cabbage, the Brussels sprout plant is very hardy and able to withstand low temperatures, so transplants can be set out 3-4 weeks before the last spring frost. In extremely warm weather, sprouts soften and spread apart.

Plants require 80-100 days from transplanting until the first sprouts mature. Transplant when 7-8 weeks old. Suggested varieties include: Catskill, Fancy Most 50-A, Alcazar, Lunet Hybrid, Jade Cross, and Long Island Improved.

Sprouts form in the axis of each leaf on the plant and are clustered around the main erect stem. You can harvest for a month or more, as the sprouts mature from the bottom of the plant upward. Pick the sprouts when they are green and hard, 1-2 inches in diameter, and before the outer leaves start to yellow. Break away the leaf just below the sprout and snap off the sprout. Always leave the top leaves: The plant needs them to supply nourishment. Harvest upward along the stem to the point where the sprouts are too small. Allow these small sprouts to remain on the stem for further development.

CABBAGE (*Brassica oleracea capitata*)

There are dozens of varieties of cabbage for the home gardener to choose from, varying in color from light green to deep reddish purple, in shape from flat to round to pointed, with leaves that are either smooth or crinkled. Among the most popular are Copenhagen Market, All Seasons, Bravo, Early Round Dutch, Meteor, Early Jersey Wakefield, Head Start, King Cole, Danish Ballhead, Red Acre, Sun-Up, Premium Flat Dutch, Red Head, Savoy Chieftain, Mammoth Red Rock, and Golden Acre.

Transplants can be ready for the table in 55-70 days. Harvest when heads are fairly firm and well filled. Pull the entire plant up by the root, then cut off the head; or cut off the head, leaving the root in the ground. If allowed to overmature, heads may split and discolor.

Planting two or more varieties of differing maturities—for example, a fast and a slow maturing one—can extend the harvest season from a week or so to a month or more. The plants do well in cold weather, with some able to withstand temperatures of 15-20° F.

CAULIFLOWER (*Brassica oleracea botrytis*)

Cauliflower grows best in cool, fairly moist climates. Plants are ready for transplanting 4-8 weeks after seeding, or seeds can be sown directly in the garden. Some early producers may be grown as both a fall and spring crop, forming good heads within 60 days after transplanting. For a longer harvest, plant or set seedlings with differing maturities—one early and one later. Popular varieties of cauliflower include: Snowball, Snow King, Snow Crown, Self Blanch, and Snowflower.

Adequate moisture is essential for normal, rapid, uniform cauliflower growth. Dryness may cause premature development and small heads. When heads are 2-4 inches across, protect the "curd" from direct exposure to the sun by gathering the longest leaves together over the curd and tying with soft twine, raffia, or tape. Called "blanching," this will also shield developing heads from damage by frost. Self Blanch and some other varieties have leaves which grow naturally to protect tender heads.

In warm weather, heads may mature in as little as 3-5 days after blanching. In cooler weather, maturity may take as long as 2 weeks. The appearance of the curd is the best guide to readiness for harvest. The heads should be of good size—usually 5-6 inches in diameter— compact, and clear white. If heads overmature, they will segment or spread apart, the surface will become fuzzy, and they will discolor.

COLLARDS (*Brassica oleracea acephala*)

The name for this member of the family *cruciferae* is a colloquial form of "colewort." The plants are grown and used like cabbage, though they do not form heads, but large rosettes of leaves which are sometimes blanched by tying together as with cauliflower. Popular varieties include: Vates, Morris Heading, Georgia, Cabbage-Collard, and Green Glaze.

Grown year-round in the South, collards are both spring and fall crops in the North. They can be seeded in the garden 4-6 weeks before the last spring frost and 6-8 weeks before the first frost in the fall. Barring sudden cold spells, collards can survive at the same low temperatures as cabbage.

Collards can grow to a height of 3-4 feet. Immature leaves are ready for harvest in as little as 40 days, mature plants in about 75 days. When harvesting, the entire *young* plant may be cut off at ground level, the entire *mature* plant may be cut off at ground level, or bottom leaves may be stripped off the plant periodically, leaving buds to grow and produce more leaves. With the latter method, spring-planted collards may be harvested throughout the summer and into winter.

Collards are said to improve in flavor as cool weather comes on, so many gardeners do not harvest the fall crop until after the first frost. Left on the plant, leaves remain tender and edible for several weeks after they reach maturity or full size.

KALE (*Brassica oleracea acephala*)

A nonheading member of *BROCCOLI & COMPANY*, kale is a cool-season biennial plant grown for its succulent curly green or greenish purple leaves. Some varieties reach 5-6 feet in height, but those grown in home gardens are usually shorter dwarf strains.

Kale is resistant to cold. It can go on producing even after freezing weather has set in; seeds may be sown 4-6 weeks before the last killing frost in the spring, and 6-8 weeks before the first killing frost in the fall. Some of the best garden varieties are Vates Blue Curled, Premier, Siberian Improved, Dwarf Blue Scotch, and Dwarf Siberian.

If seedlings are not thinned, you may harvest young plants after 40 days by cutting off just above ground level. If you have thinned and spaced plants you may want to harvest lower leaves only, starting at 50–60 days. Leave buds to form more leaves for successive cuttings.

KOHLRABI (*Brassica oleracea gongylodes*)

Kohlrabi—from a German word meaning cabbage-turnip—is variously described as a turnip that got its directions wrong, with the bulb above the ground instead of under it; and as a turnip growing on a cabbage root. The flavor is delicate; the texture is reminiscent of water chestnut. The leaves are attached to the edible turnip-like bulb. Popular varieties include Grand Duke, Purple Vienna, and Early White Vienna.

Cold resistant like all *cruciferae*, kohlrabi is easily grown from seed sown directly in the garden, though plants can be started indoors and transplanted. It matures in 45-60 days from seeding. Plant in early spring for summer harvest and again in midsummer for fall harvest, or make successive plantings.

When bulbs are 1 ½-2 inches in diameter, remove from stems by cutting off just below the bulbs.

MUSTARD (*Brassica juncea crispifolia*)

A cool climate is best for producing mustard greens. Unlike most members of *BROCCOLI & COMPANY*, mustard is an annual, grown for its long dark green edible leaves. Home garden varieties include: Southern Giant Curled, Savannah, Fordhook Fancy, Tendergreen, Florida Broadleaf, and Green Wave.

Plant seeds directly in the garden 4-6 weeks before the last frost in the spring and 6-8 weeks before the first frost in the fall. Plants are fast growing and short-lived, maturing in 35-40 days. When leaves are 6-8 inches long, harvest by cutting the whole plant off just above ground level.

Successive sowings every two weeks are recommended to provide a continuous supply. In warm weather, the plants quickly go to seed when they have matured.

RUTABAGA (*Brassica campestris napobrassica*)

Called "swedes" in some areas and "Canadian turnips" in others, biennial rutabagas were developed in ancient times from a cross between turnip and cabbage. Though resembling a turnip in shape, texture, and taste, the rutabaga takes longer to mature, stores longer, has fewer prickly leaves, firmer flesh, and more beta-carotene than turnips, and the bulbs of most are pale gold in color. Good varieties include: American Purple Top, Laurentian, White Swede, and Sweet Russian.

Seeds should be planted directly in the garden in early spring and midsummer, with maturity in 90-95 days. Harvest when roots are 3-5 inches in diameter by pulling the whole plant. The bulbs are slow to lose quality after maturing and can be left in the ground until it freezes for digging when needed. Cover thickly with leaves or straw to prevent frost damage.

TURNIP (*Brassica campestris rapa*)

Natives of Asia which are annuals when planted early and biennials when planted late in the summer, turnips thrive in cool weather. They are usually grown for harvest in the spring and fall with seed sown directly in the garden 3-4 weeks before spring's last killing frost and 7-8 weeks before fall's first killing frost. As a general rule, sow seeds to be used for greens thickly and then thin, leaving all but the greens to develop as a root crop.

Popular varieties include: White Lady, White Milan, Purple Top White Globe, Just Right, White Egg, Royal Crown, Tokyo Cross, Shoigoin, Alltop, and Seven Top, the latter three for greens only.

Greens can be cut from the plants as soon as they have developed to a usable size. Roots mature in 35-70 days and are harvested by pulling the entire plant. For highest quality, harvest when roots are 2-3 inches in diameter before they become bitter, sharp, pithy, or woody.

During late fall and early winter, turnip roots may be left in the garden and dug as needed. When really cold weather is expected, cover the plants with straw or leaves to prevent freezing.

PLANTING STEPS

1. Sow seeds in a flat or hotbed and cover with 1/2 inch of soil. Seeds germinate best at temperatures of 65° to 75° F. You can lower the temperature by ventilation or raise the temperature by using a transparent cover (plastic or glass).

2. Plant seedlings 2 to 3 inches apart in a second flat. Use a pencil or small dibble to make the planting holes.

3. Use a pencil or small dibble to remove seedlings from a flat or hotbed.

4. When transplanting young plants to the garden, take up some soil with each plant as you remove it from the flat. Use a trowel for making the planting holes. Lightly firm the soil around each plant and then water gently.

Excerpted from CES Leaflet No. 2989, *Home Vegetable Gardening.*

PLANTING DATES

(Range of dates for safe spring planting of vegetables in the open)

Last Freeze	Broccoli*	Brussels* Sprouts	Cabbage*	Cauliflower*	Collards*	Kale	Kohlrabi	Mustard	Rutabaga	Turnip
1/30	1/1-30	1/1-30	1/1-1/15	1/1-2/1	1/1-2/15	1/1-2/1	1/1-2/1	1/1-3/1		1/1-3/1
2/8	1/1-30	1/1-30	1/1-2/10	1/1-2/1	1/1-2/15	1/10-2/1	1/10-2/1	1/1-3/1		1/1-3/1
2/18	1/15-2/15	1/15-2/15	1/1-2/25	1/10-2/10	1/1-3/15	1/20-2/10	1/20-2/10	2/15-4/15		1/10-3/1
2/28	2/1-3/1	2/1-3/1	1/15-2/25	1/20-2/20	1/15-3/15	2/1-20	2/1-20	2/1-3/1	1/1-2/1	1/20-3/1
3/10	2/15-3/15	2/15-3/15	1/25-3/1	2/1-3/1	2/1-4/1	2/10-3/1	2/10-3/1	2/10-3/15	1/15-2/15	2/1-3/1
3/20	2/15-3/15	2/15-3/15	2/1-3/1	2/10-3/10	2/15-5/1	2/20-3/10	2/20-3/10	2/20-4/1	1/15-3/1	2/10-3/10
3/30	3/1-20	3/1-20	2/15-3/10	2/20-3/20	3/1-6/1	3/1-20	3/1-4/1	3/1-4/15	2/1-3/1	2/20-3/20
4/10	3/15-4/15	3/15-4/15	3/1-4/1	3/1-3/20	3/1-6/1	3/10-4/1	3/10-4/10	3/10-4/20		3/1-4/1
4/20	3/25-4/20	3/25-4/20	3/10-4/1	3/15-4/20	3/10-6/1	3/20-4/10	3/20-5/1	3/20-5/1		3/10-4/1
4/30	4/1-5/1	4/1-5/1	3/15-4/10	4/10-5/10	4/1-6/1	4/1-20	4/1-5/10	4/1-5/10	5/1-6/1	3/20-5/1
5/10	4/15-6/1	4/15-6/1	4/1-5/15	4/15-5/15	4/15-6/1	4/10-5/1	4/10-5/15	4/15-6/1	5/1-6/1	4/1-6/1
5/20	5/1-6/15	5/1-6/15	5/1-6/15	5/10-6/15	5/1-6/1	4/20-5/10	4/20-5/20	5/1-6/30	5/1-20	4/15-6/1
5/30	5/10-6/10	5/10-6/10	5/10-6/15	5/20-6/1	5/10-6/1	5/1-30	5/1-30	5/10-6/30	5/10-20	5/1-6/15
6/10	5/20-6/10	5/20-6/10	5/20-6/1	6/1-6/15	5/20-6/1	5/15-6/1	5/15-6/1	5/20-6/30	5/20-6/1	5/15-6/15
8/30	5/1-6/1	5/1-6/1	5/1-6/1	5/1-6/1	5/15-6/15	5/15-6/15	5/15-6/15	5/15-7/15	5/15-6/15	5/15-6/15
9/10	5/1-6/1	5/1-6/1	5/1-6/1	5/1-7/1	5/15-6/15	5/15-6/15	6/1-7/1	5/15-7/15	5/1-6/15	6/1-7/1
9/20	5/1-6/15	5/1-6/15	5/1-6/15	5/1-7/1	5/15-6/15	6/1-7/1	6/1-7/15	6/1-8/1	6/1-7/1	6/1-7/15
9/30	6/1-30	6/1-30	6/1-7/10	5/10-7/15	6/15-7/15	6/15-7/15	6/15-7/15	6/15-8/1	6/1-7/1	6/1-8/1
10/10	6/15-7/15	6/15-7/15	6/1-7/15	6/1-7/25	7/1-8/1	7/1-8/1	7/1-8/1	7/15-8/15	6/15-7/15	7/1-8/1
10/20	7/1-8/1	7/1-8/1	7/1-20	7/1-8/5	7/15-8/15	7/15-8/15	7/15-8/15	8/1-9/1	7/10-20	7/15-8/15
10/30	7/1-8/15	7/1-8/15	8/1-9/1	7/15-8/15	8/1-9/15	7/15-9/1	8/1-9/1	8/15-10/15	7/15-8/1	8/1-9/15
11/10	8/1-9/1	8/1-9/1	9/1-15	8/1-9/1	8/15-10/1	8/1-9/15	8/15-9/15	8/15-11/1	7/15-8/15	8/1-9/15
11/20	8/1-9/15	8/1-9/15	9/1-12/1	8/1-9/15	8/25-11/1	8/15-10/15	9/1-10/15	8/15-11/1	7/15-8/15	9/1-10/15
11/30	8/1-10/1	8/1-10/1	9/1-12/31	8/15-10/10	9/1-12/1	9/1-12/1	9/1-12/1	9/1-12/1	8/1-9/1	9/1-11/15
12/10	8/1-11/1	8/1-11/1	9/1-12/31	9/1-10/20	9/1-12/31	9/1-12/31	9/15-12/31	9/1-12/1	9/1-11/15	10/1-12/1
12/20	9/1-12/1	9/1-12/1	9/1-12/31	9/15-11/1	9/1-12/31	9/1-12/31	9/1-12/31	9/15-12/1	10/15-11/15	10/1-12/31

*Plants

SAMPLE GARDEN PLAN (15 ft x 15 ft)
WITH SUGGESTED BED WIDTHS

———————————————— 15′ ————————————————

GREEN ONIONS	BEETS	LEAF LETTUCE	
BUSH BEANS			18 in

X   X   X   X   X   X   X   X   X   X   X   X   X   X   X

| BROCCOLI | CABBAGE | CAULIFLOWER | BRUSSELS SPROUTS 2 ft |

X   X   X   X   X   X   X   X   X   X   X   X   X   X   X

BUSH WINTER SQUASH

WALKWAY

| SPINACH | MUSTARD GREENS | BUSH SUMMER SQUASH | 18 in |
| GREEN ONIONS | COLLARDS | | |

   X   X   X   X   X   X   X   X

| EGGPLANT | PEPPERS | | |

   X   X   X   X   X   X   X   X   X

| KALE | TURNIPS | BULB ONIONS | 2 ft |

WALKWAY

STAKED TOMATOES	HEAD LETTUCE	
BUSH BEANS		2 ft
STAKED TOMATOES	PEAS	

BUSH BEANS	HEAD LETTUCE	
BROCCOLI	RUTABAGA	2 ft
KOHLRABI		

	HERBS	2 ft

INDEX

Oh, thrice and four times happy those who plant cabbages!
—Rabelais

_____